LANDTDAGSHUSET, THE PROPOSED FINNISH PARLIAMENT HOUSE. 1908

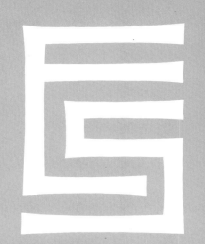

ELIEL SAARINEN

FINNISH-AMERICAN ARCHITECT AND EDUCATOR

BY ALBERT CHRIST-JANER

WITH A FOREWORD BY ALVAR AALTO

REVISED EDITION

THE UNIVERSITY OF CHICAGO PRESS

CHICAGO AND LONDON

The University of Chicago Press, Chicago 60637
The University of Chicago Press, Ltd., London

84 85 86 87 88 89 90 91 92 93   5 4 3 2

Library of Congress Cataloging in Publication Data

Christ-Janer, Albert, 1910–
   Eliel Saarinen: Finnish-American architect and
educator.
   Includes bibliographies and index.
   1. Saarinen, Eliel, 1873–1950.
NA737.S3C5   1979   720'.92'4 [B]   79–832
ISBN 0–226–10464–8 (cloth)
       0–226–10465–6 (paper)

TO PIPSAN

CONTENTS

ILLUSTRATIONS

FOREWORD

I WAS NINE YEARS OLD when first I saw the work of Eliel Saarinen. It was on an early winter morning in a town imbedded in the depth of northern Finland's snow—a town of only thirty-two hundred inhabitants.

The mail, brought by the train which had come from the south, lay on the family living room table. From among the newspapers and letters I selected a magazine which caught my eye, an attractive, red-covered periodical with a heraldic lion decorating the cover, *The Young Finland*. It contained, if my memory holds, an article on rare books in the Vatican Library, a few Finnish poems, an essay on my country's folklore, and two pages of colored pictures—architectural illustrations.

Hardly any text at all accompanied these pictures, only the word "Interior" in the lower left corner and the name "Eliel Saarinen" in the lower right.

It was quite an ordinary winter morning; I can remember nothing else unusual about it. The impression made upon me by those architectural drawings was indelible. I became aware, so early, of the work of Eliel Saarinen.

It is difficult for a modern reader, European or American, who is used to elaborate weekly or monthly magazines to get a right notion of the interest that a few simple pages of pictures and printed matter could stir up. Behind this, perhaps, lies the awful question of quality versus quantity.

Just now I have before me an almost similar periodical of the year 1900. *Ateneum* is its name. It contains short writings on various cultural subjects and an article about the discoverer of the Northeast Passage, Nordenskjöld. The remainder of the magazine is devoted to Eliel Saarinen and his design of the Finnish Pavilion of the Paris World's Fair of 1900. The text is short.

In its factual summary there is only a small indication of the enthusiasm with which this masterpiece of architecture was received.

The Finnish Pavilion, set in its time, is a monument in the history of contemporary architectural design. It is a tribute still to the courageous, clear-thinking man who designed it. It says: "My creator was a pioneer."

Today much is said about "people's art" and of the spiritual relationship between the people and art. Thanks to the energies expended by the pioneers who worked with twentieth-century art forms, a significant cultural unity of people and art was achieved in Finland.

If, I, in this connection, were to mention a primary achievement of Eliel Saarinen, I would put it thus: Eliel Saarinen was helpful in eliminating some of the architectural illiteracy and some of the inferiority complexes in a country which, because of its isolation and the difficulty that outsiders encounter in learning its language, has been and still is removed from the larger cultural centers of the Western world. Finland's cultural contributions have been made primarily in terms of architecture and music—two international languages. Eliel Saarinen was a pioneer, together with Jean Sibelius, in these two art forms. Through them and their efforts the Finnish people communicated with the rest of the world.

The international success of a Finnish architect in the dawning years of the twentieth century helped his country gain self-confidence, which today, to a considerable degree, still remains the foundation of an unbending and balanced vitality which finds its outlet in hard work and in a unified cultural striving that is free from disturbing complexes.

The pioneering of Eliel Saarinen in his country eliminated the conflicts which are likely to hamper a balanced artistic production. Thanks to his honest, logical approach, the usual strife between old and new architecture does not exist in Finland. The art historian, the social reformer, the merchants, and the workers of Finland accept architecture as a self-explanatory matter, the aim of which is to clarify social functions and to make a mode of living what it ought to be.

The connoisseur, European as well as American, is familiar with Eliel Saarinen's art, with his earlier Finnish work as well as with his international achievement. There is no need to explain the clarity of his early design in times when romantic leanings steadily disturbed organic thinking. One of Eliel Saarinen's great achievements was his refusal to yield to sentimental romanticism when the general trend was toward the romantic. Nor later did he bow to pure rationalism when the move was toward the coldly rational. Students of architecture are familiar with his city plans, old and new, and they can evaluate his clear and unsentimental way of designing—a way of planning which, nonetheless, fosters sentiments of warmth and well-being.

I have tried to emphasize those things which are known best, perhaps, to those who have an intimate knowledge of Eliel Saarinen's native land. He was responsible for the contribution not only of his own work but also of even more general qualities which affected, first, his own country and then, in broader geographical circles, the area of northern Europe.

My second view of Eliel Saarinen came when I, too, went to the United States and saw him against the broader horizon of the architecture of the Western world. During my periodic visits to the Massachusetts Institute of Technology I heard many discussions about design and Eliel Saarinen's contribution to contemporary architecture.

An American friend asked me a question, a pertinent one, it seems to me, when one thinks of Eliel Saarinen and the effects of his work upon Finland.

"Is it not conceivable," queried my friend, "that, at the time just after Richardson, America and the Scandinavian countries had approximately an equal chance to build up an architecture that not only confined itself to a few scattered examples but grew to the proportions of a new environment?

"In your northerly corner of Europe," he went on to explain, "a bridge seems to have been built from that time right into our own, and along this bridge two important developments have come. First, this bridge seems to connect your architectural heritage with your present form of building, and, second, it seems to have given the architectural form a continuous chance to unify itself with your social pattern.

"The gap between Richardson's time and our own seems thus to have been spanned by a bridge that has offered you a safe crossing. Who built this bridge? Or what are the forces that created it?"

An attempt to answer this question is necessarily complicated. A few sentences will hardly do. But, in giving an answer, one must name Eliel Saarinen. He is one of the bridge builders. I would say that even in his earliest work he was constructing the bridge. The evidence is quite visible to the trained eye.

After 1923 Eliel Saarinen worked in the United States. When we compare his first period in Finland with one in America, we find the two periods to be equal in length of time.

The first stage in Finland, because of the smaller circumstances, may be called a "laboratory period," when Eliel Saarinen tested his ideas under close personal observation. Equipped with the lessons that he had learned in these experiments, he stepped out of the laboratory, one might say, into his productive period in America.

In a larger environment, faced with larger architectural problems, he created the greater part of his work. There Eliel Saarinen achieved a form suited to a new culture. This form has an abiding quality.

ALVAR AALTO

HELSINKI, FINLAND
1946

PREFACE

THIS REVISION of Eliel Saarinen's biography, first published in 1948, two years before his death, is essentially the book that he and his wife Loja both approved. Materials from their files document its pages; their recollections color its narrative.

In accord with his conviction that the nature of the man is the wellspring of production, Eliel Saarinen's background is described. His parentage, the northern environment in which he grew up, his education and his professional development, his marriage and family relationships, his response to his adopted country, his contributions as an educator, and his collaboration with his son Eero are here recorded.

"If there will be continuing interest in what I have done," he often said as we worked together to sift these facts and to interpret them meaningfully, "I want this to be the record; let time be the judge of it."

Drafts of this text were written in Eliel Saarinen's Cranbrook studio in 1946. During that year, my calendar shows, we spent 148 afternoons together, he recalling and reminiscing, selecting and editing, and I questioning, amalgamating, and recording. At five o'clock he would have tired of detailing these personal recollections and professional developments; his slightly slanted, deeply hooded blue eyes would sparkle and he would say with relief, "Ah, the cocktail hour, the happiest hour of the day. Loja, now we can have our martinis!"

During the next hours the Saarinens, refreshed, would recount anecdotes about their home and family life and describe their professional problems, debating all the while the advisability of including this or rejecting that. These sessions, of course, were both exhilarating and exacting experiences. The material thus accumulated for this biography, enriched by their discerning and concerned opinions, naturally influenced my initial manuscript, which was subjective and yet peculiarly engaging. Eliel and Loja Saarinen were inimitable!

The finished pages were later examined to fix the facts; their interpretation was corroborated; their number was reduced. In 1947 a restricted, essential text was delivered to the University of Chicago Press. It was published in 1948.

A Finnish edition was published by the Otava Press in Helsinki in 1951. In that translation part 1, covering the first half of Eliel Saarinen's architectural career before he moved to the United States, was enlarged. Designs and buildings of particular interest to citizens in his native land were added, with supplementary paragraphs. Part 2, supervised by Eero and Loja Saarinen, included Eliel Saarinen's last two years and brought his story to a close. Because of the guidance it offers for the completion of this edition, the authenticity of the record of those years is assured.

Insofar as its content was authenticated by him, this book may be regarded as the official biography of Eliel Saarinen; its revision has recently been examined by his daughter Pipsan. Joseph N. Lacy, his architectural associate from 1947 to 1950, advised in the formation of the concluding chapters.

Part 1 of this edition contains insertions of the words of a number of lifelong Finnish friends; they enrich Eliel Saarinen's portrait as a young man. For example, form and color are supplied by Professor J. S. Sirén, for many years head of the Department of Architecture at the Institute of Technology in Helsinki, a man who knew him for forty years. Excerpts in free translation, supplied by Loja Saarinen in 1955, are taken from Professor Sirén's address, delivered at the opening of the Memorial Exhibition of Eliel

Saarinen's work, in June of that year.

Part 2 includes those plans and buildings which, in the first edition, were shown under the heading "Work in Progress," but were completed after 1947. The most noted of these is the General Motors Technical Center in Warren, Michigan. However, after consultation with those who helped to complete this vast work, which was dedicated in 1956, it was decided to show mainly the concept which the elder Saarinen first proposed; what was finally constructed was really Eero's design.

Excerpts from the memorial service, with praise from the Premier of Finland and eloquent, touching homage from Eliel Saarinen's famed Finnish successor, Alvar Aalto, close this volume.

When Douglas Haskell, dean of editors, who maintained the distinguished *Architectural Forum* for so many years, discussed this revision, he said, "Eliel Saarinen was monumental. And then another generation, Eero's, came along which already seems to have lived in yet another age. Now even Eero's generation is challenged by the Venturi crowd." True, the elder Saarinen's concepts are just what Venturiism would reject as being "too heroic, boring and expensive." Turn to the rendering across from the title page, Landtdagshuset, for an illustration of what seems impossible these days, if not downright undesirable.

The disruption of established values—social and philosophical, economic and aesthetic—since Eliel Saarinen covered his drafting board for the last time has affected architecture fundamentally. The span of decades between him and Robert Venturi, a designer with energetic intelligence and glittering talent, whose display at the Whitney Museum of American Art in the fall of 1971 caused much controversy, is longer than one fully realizes until those rapidly changing years are scrutinized.

Obviously Eliel Saarinen's creations are of another period. The young architect who examines Saarinen's plans, designs, and buildings, his sumptuous materials erected so fastidiously, his lavish employment of space, and his soaring monumentality may well be incredulous or even scornful. For as Professor Sirén sensitively expressed it, "In his loftiest moments, such creations were a

great festivity, for which he presented himself in full dress with white tie; of course, and above all, it meant work."[1] Not one of his successors that I know owns a white tie nor would he wear one; neither does he have a bent for the heroic.

Examined in the light of Venturiism, Eliel Saarinen's visions and achievements are, perhaps, remote. The speed of change in architectural concepts since he died has produced a chorus of clamoring voices which condemn or, more likely, ignore the work of those who aspired to the monumental. Therefore most of Eliel Saarinen's work may seem out of place in this world; some might say so regretfully, others thankfully.

During the critical intervening years since the first biography of Eliel Saarinen was published, a rejective attitude toward tradition has raged. Nowhere has it appeared more disturbing than in building; out of this turmoil new forms have been produced from new ideas.

The lively movement that Robert Venturi, his wife Denise Brown Scott, and their associates set going seems to be one which, logically and productively, is on the very opposite end of the value line from where Eliel Saarinen stood. Venturi's and Reyner Banham's ideas offer attainable solutions to an increasing number of restive designers and builders who are attracted by their vernacular. Venturiism is for many young architects a vanguard banner,[2] but others would agree with critic Robert Hughes, "Trash may be language, but it remains trash."

If the Las Vegas Strip and Levittown are indeed the future of building, Eliel Saarinen will remain where some of his successors have placed him—in the museum. But while Venturiism may allure today's commercial predators for profit, it may not be the answer to our heart's deepest desire. *Ars longa, vita brevis,* even now. The heroic may not be dead, though it be a trial to

1. This is the first of a number of quotations taken from the main address given by Professor Sirén, at the opening of the memorial exhibition of Eliel Saarinen's work in Helsinki, June 1, 1955. Others will be found throughout part 1.

2. See the Whitney Museum of American Art's brochure: "The Work of Venturi and Rauch" for a commentary by Vincent J. Scully, Jr., on the exhibition they supplied in the fall in 1971. Also Tician Papachristou and James Stewart Polchek, "Venturi: Style Not Substance?" *New York Times,* November 14, 1971. The first tends to be positive, the second, negative.

build and difficult and expensive to maintain. Is it impossible?

Because heroic expression in architecture rears up again and again in man's cultural history, it will most likely continue to be designed and built in spite of cost and burdens of maintenance. It is a necessity of the human spirit. Eliel Saarinen and Robert Venturi indeed reflect the extremes of man's views of himself and his destiny.

This biography is being published so that those who have continuing faith in splendid concepts, who may themselves wish to strike out for what seems unattainable, can become acquainted with a precursor. While some designers, roused by the present complex and pressing human condition, "refuse both to take refuge in a style or trouble to invent a fresh one," as Vincent Scully put it, others will be inspired to build on foundations offered by those who rejected imitation to invent imaginatively. The creations of Eliel Saarinen, never slavish and ever inventive, furnished stones for that foundation.

Would Eliel Saarinen have shut his eyes to change? He could not have ignored the universal quandary. How would he have reacted to the relentless force that shakes this latter half of the twentieth century?

In light of his lifelong devotion to education, an artist among artists in Europe and America, Eliel Saarinen would have adapted his ideas and techniques, both as an educator and designer. During his last year, I once asked him, "On the basis of your life as an architect—just a quarter of a century in Finland and exactly that length of time here in the United States—what would you predict about the future of architecture?"

"In my crystal ball," he replied, his light blue eyes glinting through tilted, half-closed lids, "I see that during the next half of the century the time of collaboration between the clients, the financier, the lawyer, the politician and the architect-planner will be required to meet the manifold problems which lurk ahead. The heyday of 'signed' architecture is over." He foresaw the development of teams of designers who would pool their knowledge with allied fields, combining their political and financial power to meet the future demand. In conversation he often commended Walter Gropius for his leadership in

forming creative units among the associates in his office. But he would not have acclaimed the commonplace.

Eliel Saarinen's considered opinion about the shape and demand of the future is stated in *The City* (1943), which he was revising when we worked together.[3]

During his last evaluation of the enormous difficulty that besets the planner who aims to encompass in his design an area sufficient to be considered seriously as even a partial solution to the immediate problem, Eliel Saarinen said, "Architecture embraces the whole form-world of man's physical accommodations, from the intimacy of his room to the comprehensive labyrinth of the large metropolis. Within this broad field of creative activities, the architect's ambition must be to develop a form language expressing the *best* aims of *his time*—and of no other time— and to cement the various features of his expressive forms into a good interrelation, and ultimately into the rhythmic coherence of the multiformed organism of the city."

While Eliel Saarinen would not have accepted Woodward Avenue in Detroit as the highway to the future, he would not have repeated himself by drawing up monumental concepts he once dreamed up for the new city of Canberra. While he would not have settled for Las Vegas, he would not have been indifferent to what architectural critics like Peter Blake see as the new form of the complex which will accommodate the involved activities of the burgeoning community.

Insofar as it reveals his own time and its conditions, Eliel Saarinen's work is significant. His forms contributed to his culture. His work, selectively illustrated on these generous pages, enriched the modern tradition. Insofar as it was associated with history, in which Eliel Saarinen was constantly absorbed and broadly informed, his ideas concerning his work are often quoted. Either he spoke to me about them or they were taken from the manuscript of his book *Search for Form: A Fundamental Approach to Art,* upon which he was at work when we planned this biography.

This text is pared and expositive; it depicts the

3. The revised edition was published in 1965.

subject with outline strokes, with some risk of adumbration; no final judgments are attempted.

However, when comments by reviewers and critics provided desirable explanation or contributed pertinent commentary about Eliel Saarinen or his work, they are quoted.

Most important, Eliel Saarinen speaks for himself in his designs. The main purpose, therefore, of this picture book is to display architectural plans, renderings, and photographs. (Since 1955 the assembled work of Eliel Saarinen has been housed in the architectural museum of Helsinki.) To those who are interested in his own analytical studies of city and environmental planning and in his concepts of form in art, his two volumes *The City* and *The Search for Form* are recommended.

Eliel Saarinen made his contribution to design—an international language, which he spoke with a highly personal accent. During all the periods of his creative life he constantly explored form.

But form is ever challenging. Eliel Saarinen recognized its elusive qualities. He accepted this challenge and won his place among the creative artists of his time.

1972   ALBERT CHRIST-JANER
Fuller E. Callaway Professor of Art
University of Georgia

Because of delays too numerous to mention, the publication of this completed life of Eliel Saarinen has been held up six years. Were Albert writing today, parts of it, perhaps the preface, might assume a slightly different tone, or some of his observations might be endowed with additional years of perspective.

He would be delighted, for instance, to learn that the Saarinen's home at Cranbrook is now being restored. No guest there will ever forget its expressiveness. It personified the entwined lives of two individuals who had studied, talked about, and worked with the forms of art for their entire lifetime. Everything one saw, or touched, or heard had to do with their sense of design, of form-expression, of the underlying meaning of whatever was at hand. It was a great, enriching experience to know the Saarinens so intimately; listening to their recollections, working with their records introduced us to the largest, and the smallest, implications of art.

I hope that Albert's aim of presenting a straightforward account of Saarinen's life may be regarded as a faithful attempt to sum up the achievements of a creative architect and planner. Eliel Saarinen, Aalto's bridge builder, finished his work in 1950; time will judge the length and strength of his span.

1979   VIRGINIA CHRIST-JANER

1   ELIEL SAARINEN. 1945. " 'Work is the key to creative growth of mind . . .' " *Photo by C.A.A.*

PART ONE

1

On August 20, 1873, a child was born to Pastor Juho and Selma Broms Saarinen in Rantasalmi, Finland. At the Lutheran baptismal ceremony the boy was named Gottlieb Eliel. He was always called Eliel.

In the modest parsonage in which Eliel grew up his dedicated parents served their congregation; they were required to tend to the daily needs of the poor who lived in harsh circumstances. The earth, hard and cold, did not yield crops easily nor abundantly. Toil and striving sustained the hardy Northman; only by self-denial could he survive the long, white winters.

On isolated homesteads the farmers wrested their living from forest clearings, from wasted flatlands, and from the streams and lakes. Each home was built and sustained by hands with many skills. These hands tied the knots and plied the seines of fishermen, loaded the guns and baited the traps of hunters, and plowed and reaped. Flax and wool were made into sturdy materials which the women cut and sewed. Hands with deft fingers were the servants of necessity.

For generations the Finn had been a man of all work who learned his skills and sharpened his wits in his daily labor. Thus, from youth, the men and women of the north were trained to cope with their environment, in the forest and on the plain, on sea and on land.

Each man's duties, demanding his devotion, gave him strength and dignity. He used this strength to master his environment, and it, in turn, gave him mastery over himself.

To such people Pastor Juho Saarinen offered his services. Not only did he know the immediate needs of his congregation, but in his studies he developed an understanding of the historical tragedy of his native land: for centuries Finland has been a buffer between powerful, opposing forces.

How frequently and with what pain his country had borne the brunt of the collision of powers concentrated on her left and right was a story that Pastor Saarinen knew well. As he read the history of northern Europe, he realized that once, on September 17, 1809, a hope had lived in the hearts of his ancestors. At the Treaty of Fredrikshamn, the exhausted Swedes made a decisive commitment to Russia by ceding all rights to Finland and the Åland Islands, thus ending five centuries of struggle.

Ironically, the Finns found in Russia the foster-mother of their nationality. In attempting to stamp out Swedish influence, the Russians encouraged the people of Finland to create a cultural unity. Alexander I, who made possible the treaty of 1809, and Alexander II, who convoked the Finnish Diet in 1863, were directly responsible for the unification of modern Finland.

With the pledge of Alexander I in 1809 at the convention of the four Estates of the realm at Borga, where he promised to "confirm and ratify the religion and fundamental laws of the country," the union of Finland with Russia became a contract in which Finland's constitution was to be respected.

Until 1809 Finland had remained undeveloped as a nation, although many leaders, poets, and thinkers were aware of her potential wealth. There had been no unity in the spoken language. The Svekomans, who represented aristocratic, sophisticated cultural trends, spoke only Swedish; the Fennomans, who sought the roots of Finnish culture deep in the soil, spoke Finnish. With Ivar Arvidsson, the Fennomans said: "We have ceased to be Swedes; we cannot be Russians; therefore we must be Finns."

With the longing for national identity, the need for education was recognized. In the words of the statesman-philosopher J. W. Snellman: "We Finns are few in number; we must make strength of our weakness by widespread enlightenment." To this great task of education Pastor Juho Saarinen devoted his life.

The key to the problem of general education lay, of course, in the development of a national literature. Rough vernacular was shaped into a medium that was to express the people's literary inheritance. A dictionary was compiled. The national epic was collected in 1853. Elias Lönnrot contributed a treasure to Finland's cultural store when, in 1849, he arranged a collection of the old ballads into a connected poem, *Kalevala*. Much in the manner in which the *Iliad* and the *Odyssey* are thought to have been put together by order of Pisistratus, Lönnrot edited the *Kalevala*, based on the ancient songs of Finland. Its form later became the model for Henry Wadsworth Longfellow's *Hiawatha* and *Evangeline*.

The gray cold hues of her winter, the brilliance of her green spring, the vital swiftness of fleeting summer, and the hoar of autumn are beautiful areas of a mosaic which depict the life of the northern people. From this folk hoard the northland can be known (*Kalevala, the Land of Heroes*, tr. W. F. Kirby [London: Dent, 1923–25], 1:1–3):

Let us clasp our hands together,
Let us interlock our fingers;
Let us sing a cheerful measure,
Let us use our best endeavour,
While our dear ones hearken to us,
And our loved ones are instructed;
While the young are standing round us,
Of the rising generation,
Let them learn the words of magic,
And recall our songs and legends.
. . . .

These my father sang aforetime,
As he carved his hatchet's handle,
And my mother taught me likewise,
As she turned around her spindle.
. . . .

There are many other legends;
Songs I learned of magic import;
Some beside the pathway gathered;
Others broken from the heather;

Others wrested from the bushes;
Others taken from the saplings,
Gathered from the springtime verdure,
Or collected from the by-ways,
As I passed along as herd-boy,
As a child in cattle-pastures,
On the hillocks, rich in honey,
On the hills, forever golden.
. . . .

Is the ball to be unravelled
And the bundle's knot unfastened?
Then I'll sing so grand a ballad,
That it wondrously shall echo,
While the rye-bread I am eating,
And the beer of barley drinking,
But though ale should not be brought me,
And though beer should not be offered,
I will sing, though dry my throttle,
Or will sing, with water only,
To enhance our evening's pleasure,
Celebrate the daylight's beauty
Or the beauty of the daybreak,
When another day is dawning.

For such a cultural monument as the *Kalevala*, for the spiritual unification of the nation, Finland paid a price. During the latter part of the nineteenth century the Finnish-Swedish differences in language and customs were not resolved. The Svekomans pointed out the consequences if the Swedish language, intimately associated with the European family, were to be supplanted by Finnish; in return, the Fennomans asserted that the nation could find expression only in a national language. The dilemma was stated briefly, "My intellect is with the Svekomans, but my emotions are with the Fennomans." Internal conflict was bitter. Finland has never escaped the heat of two fires, either culturally or politically.

While the Finnish cultural movement was progressing, the political promise was not so happily fulfilled. During the first half of the nineteenth century the Diet failed to convene. In 1863, Czar Alexander II called a conference of the four Estates—the nobles, the clergy, the burgesses, and the peasants. A constitutional monarchy would be maintained as "essentially involved in the character of the Finnish people." The Diet convened quite regularly after 1863, and the Finns enjoyed a healthy degree of freedom in their national institutions until the end of the century.

When a new spirit of Pan-Slavism surged up in Russia, the Finns, who had been applying themselves diligently to the arts of peace, were grievously upset. In 1898, a radical departure from previous Russian policy was announced by the czar; the Diet was rendered impotent, and imperialism made harsh demands. The Finns were filled with wrath when a malicious governor—a martinet, General Bobrikoff—issued orders for submission. They spoke their opposition bravely. When Bobrikoff was assassinated in 1904, an outbreak occurred, and sporadic acts of political violence were committed. Uncertainty and conflict reigned.

Russia, beset by her internal problems as a result of the Russo-Japanese War, made concessions to Finland in 1905. For a time there was calm. But within five years the placating agencies were removed, and the political situation again became vitally disturbed. This state of agitation continued until March, 1917, when the Diet was permitted to meet once again and the Social Democrat party came to power.

Then, threatened by the Red Russian drive for a reestablishment of revolutionary forces in Finland and with penalties which she had to pay for German intervention, Suomi, "the ancient land of the marshes," regimented her resources and stood forth in 1918 to achieve her fleeting time of independence. She paid a price of violence and death for that period of freedom, unique in her history. Finland's existence today is a magnificent tribute to her courage.

For Pastor Juho Saarinen these movements of history of his native land were as the days of his life. To further the education of his people he gave his knowledge; for the development of the culture of the Suomi he translated German texts into Finnish. At the height of the revolution, when the vines he had planted and tended were uprooted, Pastor Saarinen left his congregation in Saint Petersburg to join his son Eliel and family at Hvitträsk near Helsingfors. There he watched the daybreak of his country's period of liberty. The day came and went. But Pastor Saarinen did not live to see the time, the two decades between the great world wars, when Finland was a free, proud nation. He died in the winter of 1921.

2 SPANKKO. Watercolor. 1893. "On isolated homesteads the farmers wrested their living . . ."

3   FINNISH LANDSCAPE. Watercolor. 1893. "Dark lakes, mirrors for the hills . . ."

2

The fields of the harvesters were bounded on three sides by yellow valleys and dark-green hills; on the fourth was the sea. The summits to the north were crowned with birch woods; man's work—the straight rows of corn—flourished on the hillsides; rye, as high as a man, waved gently in the valleys. Dark lakes, mirrors for the hills, were warmed by the sun, their mysterious depth untouched.

It was in the valley that man's hand created order. The tilled soil of the homesteads at Mäntyharju yielded good crops. On the greensward, securely fenced in, herds of cows carried full udders. In other fields the sheep grazed among green clusters.

Centered among the modest houses, the church spire reared its thin shaft against the blue-green backdrop of the hills. It gave calm and reassurance to the harvester. The yards lay clean and orderly, with their simple, efficient arrangements of small barns and sheds. Clustered within an area of no more than three square miles, small homes dotted the valley; within them women worked, and around them children played. The life of the village went its slow, uneventful, domestic way.

In such an environment Eliel Saarinen was reared. As a boy he learned to love the forests and the lakes, to become more absorbed in the twist of a birch branch than in the books at school. The scenes of Finland and of the Russian territory to the south in which he spent his childhood were absorbing to the eyes of the growing boy.

4

Eliel Saarinen was the second of six children. "I was born, you see, with that predisposition for the second place," he often remarked with a wry smile, "and I have frequently had the benefits of my inheritance." His mother, a woman of quiet humor and profound religious feeling, was the solace of the community; she ministered to the sick and needy with devotion.

In his country home young Eliel learned to enjoy reading and intelligent discussion and to respect sincerity of religious thought. Of his parents, he recalled: "From them I received, above all, a love for work." From them also he received a sound body, a physical strength which never failed him.

The duties of the pastor called Juho Saarinen to various locations. He worked first in the country parish at Rantasalmi, Finland, where he learned the duties of the ministry. In those days the pastor of the church was the leader of the community.

When Eliel was two years old, Pastor Juho Saarinen received a call from the congregation at Liisilä, in Ingermanland, Russia, where he began the first of his heroic years among the isolated Lutherans of a frequently hostile land.

Two years later, in 1877, the Saarinens moved again, to Spankkova, also in Ingermanland. It was there that Pastor Saarinen spent his mature strength, working with lowly people who, not so many years before, had been serfs on the land.

In school young Eliel was not a prodigy. He was an ordinary lad, full of healthy interest in the world about him. In the Klassillinen Lyseo, which he entered at the age of ten, Eliel began his formal training, with an emphasis upon Latin and the classics. Because this course of study was not a happy one for the boy, he transferred to that section of the curriculum which stressed modern languages and the sciences. There he did well in his studies and developed his natural leanings.

Through the study of the sciences Eliel laid the foundation for his subsequent study of nature and, later, for his translation of the designs he found in nature into architectural constructions. His absorption in botanical forms was expressed in many of the drawings he made when he dreamed of becoming a painter.

The nonclassical elementary education in Viborg gave the boy some opportunities for self-realization. During his hours away from the classroom, during vacation trips, and on journeys to Saint Petersburg when he went home to visit his family, he often stopped at L'Hermitage, where he had his first sight of the works of the masters.

"This was the most significant part of my

4 PARISH HOUSE, SPANKKOVA. Watercolor. 1893. "The yards lay clean and orderly . . ."

5 RUSSIAN FARM WAGON, SPANKKOVA. Wash drawing. 1893. "In this rural setting . . . with paper and pencil . . ."

training; at least, so it seems to me in memory. My love for Rembrandt—though it may seem unusual that the Dutch master would attract my child's eye—whose qualities, which have maintained his place constantly for centuries, were impressed upon me then. I am glad this happened so, and proud, too.

"The Hermitage became my Mecca. For hours I could walk around from gallery to gallery, alone, silent, and happy; a country boy, familiar with pigs, cows, and hens, amid these most precious masterpieces of all time!

"I knew the paintings. I knew the names on the labels. Probably I was satisfied with a direct and personal relationship with these paintings. They spoke to me, or so I probably felt; I understood their speech, or so I probably thought."

At Tammerfors, Finland, Eliel entered the Realyceum, a secondary school, where art education consisted of a laborious business of copying plaster casts. It was a killing process, in Finland as anywhere else in the ordinary schools of that time, and therefore Eliel sought his drawing lessons outside the classroom. "I used my vacations and my school time—too much of my school time, I fear—in drawing the things I wished to draw and in my own way."

Eliel's teacher in drawing was persuaded by his pupil to permit representation from nature, but only after the plaster casts on the wall had

been painstakingly copied. The keys of the studio were given to Eliel, and he was granted the privilege of drawing the casts in the evenings.

Outdoor sports played a prominent part in Eliel's life at this point. He skated and went skiing during the long winters.

"After sneaking through my college entrance examinations I went to Helsingfors, where I enrolled as a student of architecture at Polytekniska Institutet, and in the university art school as a student of painting. The former was the choice of a cool mind, the latter the demand of a warm heart."

From 1893 to 1897 Eliel Saarinen worked, with divided interest, in design and in painting. The painting he saw in the studios of his contemporaries at that time was trained toward an imitative naturalism, and the young student took it for what it was; he tried his hand at such delineation and found that he could perform with cleverness. At the time such an achievement was what he could appreciate. He did not then comprehend the shallowness of this representational and impressionistic art.

Later, when he knew more about painting he said: "Rather than become a third-rate cobbler, a common craftsman, I was willing to sacrifice my dream to be a painter." It was not until 1903, when he became acquainted with Julius Meier-Graefe, who frequently visited Hvitträsk, the home of the Saarinens, that he saw the problems of modern painting as expressed by the inventive French artists.

So, with the purpose of finding a way for honest self-expression and because he was awakening to the challenge of a new architectural era, Eliel Saarinen turned to the art of design in architecture.

3

Now, there was certainly little in the architecture of this time to inspire Eliel Saarinen. "Architecture was a dead art form," he said. "It had gradually become the business of crowding obsolete and meaningless stylistic decoration on the building surface. And it was a sacrilege to break with such a procedure, which was held to be as sacred as the dogmas of religion."

How, then, did this young student of design come to the conclusion, all-important to him, that for contemporary needs his time must develop a new architectural form? The self-realization of Eliel Saarinen was a gradual development during the years from 1893 to 1900.

"The early growth of Eliel Saarinen reveals the inner relationship between personality and style. It is also convincing proof, as it always is when an artist is born, that stylistic expression is only a surface phenomenon—the impulses of the soul of the artist go deeper. The quality of expression is the constituent that decides the artistic, the ultimate value. This quality was evident during his early years," Professor Sirén, head of the Architectural Department of the Institute of Technology of Helsinki, said in his address at the opening of the Eliel Saarinen memorial exhibition in Helsinki in 1955. He spoke as one of the architect's lifelong friends.

While Eliel Saarinen, during those first years, was apparently swayed by the strong influences of the popular National Romanticism,[1] his independent spirit and his searching mind sustained him at a point short of outright rebellion, yet near that border of revolt where artists of substance thrive.

"I did all I could to get rid of the confused and academically entrenched eclecticism of my schooling and also avoid that style which, I re-

1. See Chronological Catalogue: National Museum, Helsingfors.

gret to say, was so attractive to all of us young romantics. Indeed, at the time I began to work, architecture could hardly be considered an art form at all. I often floundered but I struggled for honest expression which, I believe, I have continued to do all my life."

During this decade a productive insurgence was prompting men outside Finland to voice their rebellion, just as Saarinen was learning to declare himself. H. P. Berlage, in Amsterdam, spoke out with vehemence: "Imitation architecture is a lie. Lying is the rule, truth the exception." Louis Sullivan in Chicago stated prophetically: "Form follows function!" Henri van de Velde, from his native Belgium, felt the subtle upswell of the wave of moving time and aided the movement: "I told myself—this was in 1892 —that I would never allow my wife and family to find themselves in immoral surroundings." Frank Lloyd Wright voiced his creed: "Traditions may be kept in the letter, after the spirit has fled, only by rejecting Him." Otto Wagner, from the Academy of Vienna, wrote a small book for his students in which he stated that the opinion of the layman of this period "has been and is disastrous in its influence."

To this small but inspired chorus Eliel Saarinen joined his voice in Helsingfors: "Architecture has gone astray; something has to be done about it; now is the time to do things."

Strange as it may appear now, these men had no personal contact; they did not read their reports at a world convention of architects. Theirs were voices crying in a wilderness.

In Finland's capital there were various associations which Eliel Saarinen enjoyed and from which he gained immensely. Among the architects who, because they, too, were questioning and intelligent observers, were searching for an answer, there were two classmates, Herman Gesellius and Armas Lindgren, and also the talented Lars Sonck and the brothers Jung.

While Saarinen, Gesellius, and Lindgren were still students in Polytekniska Institutet, they established an architectural firm in Helsingfors. Herman Gesellius, an older brother of Loja Gesellius, whom Eliel Saarinen married in 1904, was a man of practical outlook; in frequent debate with Saarinen, he helped him to formulate his own ideas. In Armas Lindgren the partners found a scholar who balanced and extended the theories advanced by his associates.

6 SKETCH. 1892. " '. . . a strong urge to draw and paint . . . proved lasting and of decisive effect . . .' "

"The discussion and argument was a stimulant for me," Eliel Saarinen recalled. "I trailed along behind trying to pick up the pieces and arrange a unified pattern."

The advanced spirit of the times and the immediate influence of his environment combined to make up the answer to the question of why Eliel Saarinen made his decision to enter the field of design in architecture and why he knew from the outset that he would never compromise himself by building in a manner that he believed to be false.

The firm of Gesellius, Lindgren, and Saarinen, formed in 1896, became within a few years the leading firm of modern Finnish architecture. The situation was ripe for experimentation; the youthful partners had courage and foresight, and

they won acclaim with gratifying speed. "Before we had completed our courses at the school we had won two prizes. Then during our first years in our offices, we received an unbelievable amount of commissions," the leading partner said. Such success, as every architect knows, is not common.

The partners of the newly established firm created their designs cooperatively. It is impossible to evaluate separately the contributions of Eliel Saarinen to the firm during this period.

Upon Eliel Saarinen's graduation from Polytekniska Institutet, the year following the establishment of his architectural firm, he won a traveling scholarship. The stipulation was that the recipient should travel in Europe for one year. Saarinen, however, could not afford to take this time away from the work piled up in his office. "I went to the director and told him I could not accept, because of the stipulation, and worked my way toward the door. He called me back, though, when he saw I was in earnest, gave me a fierce look, and handed me the money."

In later trips to Germany, France, and Italy, Eliel Saarinen enjoyed pleasant vacations, but he did not then come into direct contact with the work of contemporaries who were experimenting with new forms. Thus, while he responded to the influences which travel and reading exert upon the alert mind and though he studied the isolated evidences of good contemporary buildings when he came upon them, he denied any specific influence that markedly affected his style. He still had to find his own way in his search for a form that fulfilled his demands of contemporary building for modern needs.

The first prizes that the firm of young architects won were in competitions for plans for the Tallberg apartment building in Helsingfors and for a market building in Tammerfors.

"I had a headache when we got through celebrating this first prize we won," Saarinen remembered. "You know how it might be—young fellows winning such a prize."

As he studied, Eliel Saarinen's conception of design reached out to include the crafts of Finland—metalwork, furniture, weaving, and ceramics. The architectural firm, backed by a sound conviction concerning the importance of these arts, gathered together a staff of artisans who were to create the furnishings for their buildings.

"This was my most valuable schooling. I

opened my eyes to the scope of design; before this time it was generally thought not within the architect's realm to work with the designing of furniture."

At first glance, it might appear that a connection could be shown between this idea of the members of the firm and the work of the arts and crafts associations which were flourishing in England. Such is not the case, however, for the young Finnish designers were too far away, too remote from the movement in England. A connection might be made between their work and art nouveau, which developed on the Continent. The trend in England which passed from art associations, like William Morris's early group, to the Continent in the 1880s gave impetus to the philosophy of design that later became known as art nouveau and, in Germany, the Jugendstil.

The Finnish firm opposed the style development—a mannerism of decoration for the sake of "style"—which was typical of art nouveau. But, though they were not obviously influenced by the style development, they were greatly interested in the inventive spirit of the trend. They also felt the creative forces at work in Germany.

The fundamental purpose of the members of the Helsingfors firm was to design, for comfort and aesthetic satisfaction, for utility and attractiveness, a type of furniture and of furnishings that would fulfill the demands made upon it by the intelligent consumer. Historical styles, of course, were rejected; fresh and logical patterns were created by experimentation based on common sense.

"We went back to the nature of the material and tried to find a simple and honest way of using this material," Eliel Saarinen recalled.

Years after he had forgotten the details of those commissions that the young architect received in 1898 and 1899, when he could not recall any but the main aspects of the problems that he and his colleagues tried to solve during those years, he said: "I have learned to know that, to understand art in all comprehensiveness, one must understand the world beyond the problems of art—that is, one must learn to understand life from which all art springs. And I have learned that, in order to understand both art and life, one must go down to the source of all things: to nature.

"The landscape of my childhood homeland was gentle, with flowing fields, with meadows and forests. My environment was limited and to my liking. In this rural setting I ran around, very often with paper and pencil in my hands, for I had a strong urge to draw and paint. Of course, every child has that desire, more or less, but in my case it has proved lasting and of decisive effect."

His interest in nature manifested itself throughout his school training and he tried to depict the structures he found in nature. This study, which influenced him throughout his life, was a continuous one which he felt to be essential for the evolution of a healthy design form in architecture.

The first experience that Eliel Saarinen had as an architect who sought the guidance of nature came to him while he and his associates made their search for form in designing the early buildings of their career. When making the plans for their commissions, the architects went to nature to study the materials; Eliel Saarinen awoke to new realizations of the qualities of wood and stone. With no classical design to be copied, with no shibboleths to comfort him, he studied nature with an interest prompted by need. "Material was our only guide, and because we tried to use material in its nakedness we might have been called romantic—though I hardly know how to define that word today," said Saarinen in referring to Paloniemi, a country estate he and his associates designed and built in Lojo, Finland, in 1898.

Often the young trio went astray, for youth had not yet been vested with the wisdom that comes from broad experience. Eliel Saarinen was then twenty-five years of age; his two companions were younger. So, though helped by nature, they were also frequently confused by her.

Nature did offer substantial help, however, and this aid became a marked feature of the designs the firm created during these years. Designed in 1899, Wuorio's villa at Hästnäsund, Finland, which was located in a heavily wooded countryside, featured a timber construction in keeping with its surroundings. Here the nature of material was explored, and, further, it was related to its setting in a simple and logical manner.

"We did not sit around thinking, though," said Eliel Saarinen, when he recalled these busy years. "It seems to me we worked feverishly most of the time, trying to keep our heads above the rush of work."

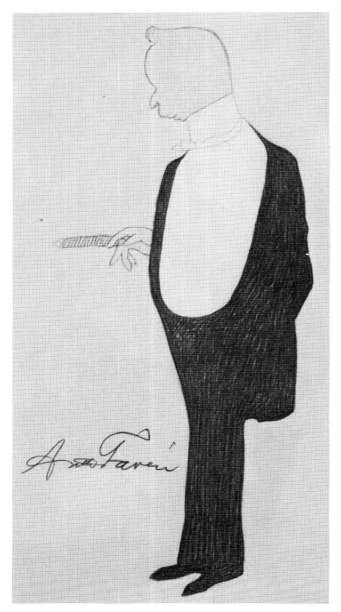

7 ELIEL SAARINEN BY ANTTI FAVÉN

The competition for the Verdandis Life Insurance Building, Åbo, Finland, in which the firm won second prize, drove the architects to an unusual effort. They received word of the competition at midnight the day before the deadline for the work submitted, and shipped out the completed drawings at eight o'clock the following morning.

There were not many such dramatic events, however. It was all in a day's work, normally, to bend over the drafting table for twelve to fifteen hours, labor which required more fortitude than heroics.

Recreational hours were spent with the group of artists concentrated in Helsingfors in the closing years of the nineteenth century. In general, these artists were forward-looking and imbued with high cultural aims. There were painters and sculptors and many interested in the crafts, for in the Nordic countries at that time handicrafts were held to be important, as they are today. There were men of letters, both Finnish and Swedish; there were musicians and composers, among them Jean Sibelius, one of the leaders of the group. "These men certainly formed the strongest, most youthful movement of the arts in the history of Finland," Saarinen said with pride.

"The world opened up," as Sirén recalls, "full of springtime promise for this young, gifted, and receptive circle. . . . The time was characterized by a forceful release of creative power, born of daring and unrestrained conviction."

A companionable young man who enjoyed the society of the various artistic and intellectual groups, Eliel Saarinen was in the center of many discussions and heated arguments about art and things in general. These associations gave him a more catholic view of life.

"There was much to enliven discussion toward the turn of the century," Saarinen recalled. "On one side there was that climax of the self-conscious stage of art development, that ivory tower of the Ecole des Beaux-Arts and of the Grand Salon. On the other was the debased taste which gradually reached as low a level as mankind had ever before experienced. And, finally, there was an ever growing dissatisfaction with existing conditions." This mood of dissatisfaction Eliel Saarinen found stimulating. Energetic, full of youthful enthusiasm, he took a firm stand against the follies of the Beaux-Arts schools; he would not tolerate the taste that was common in the era, and he was happy to add to the discontent.

Far away in Chicago, Louis Sullivan, older and more experienced, was concerned with the same questions. Over his drafting board Eliel Saarinen had tacked a photograph of the facade of the Transportation Building at the Chicago World's Fair. He was attracted by its qualities of rebellion. It was a sign to him that there was another who felt as he did; it became a symbol of the architect's search for a way to find a contemporary solution to basic problems.

It was not that Saarinen felt that Sullivan's design was a total solution. As a matter of fact, the doorway of the Transportation Building was a tour de force of decoration. But, as such, it was of high importance, for, as Walter Curt Behrendt clearly states: "The history of art proves that the advent of a new style is always announced first in a change of decoration. Because it is difficult to change the structure of building without altering economic and social relations, a new impetus first becomes visible in the agile and easily changeable art of decoration."[2] The design, expressing as it did Sullivan's adventuresome spirit, was an important step.

Saarinen and his associates, in trying to find a logical way, designed a structure which, to their great surprise, attracted wide attention. In 1899 a competition was announced for the Finnish Pavilion to be built at the Paris Exposition in 1900.[3] The opportunity offered the young architects was one they appreciated; it was a chance to solve a problem logically, without the restrictions of a client's wishes. Their design, small but purposeful, won the first award.

"Though we did not think much about it when we began the work, we realized after the prize was given us that we had our first opportunity to place our work outside Finland, and, in this sense, I should say, it was the first work of significance for us from what might be called a 'historical' viewpoint," said Eliel Saarinen.

The Finnish Pavilion was not a great work of art, but it was by far the simplest building at the exposition. What is worth noting is the state of architectural design revealed by the Paris structures. "It was a dangerous time," Saarinen reflected, "as you can see when you study the nightmares erected at Paris in 1900."

"After the ornamental sweet dreams and decorative frightfulness, the road onward seemed pretty hazy. It was a well-known fact in those days that, to pioneer, one had to be clear-headed enough to steer between the Scylla of overused classicism and the Charybdis of random forms of sparkling novelty. There were many exaggerations, many mistakes, many compromises, and many outright retreats to the old."

In the autumn of 1899 Eliel Saarinen went to Paris to supervise the building of the pavilion. Although he was depressed by the sight of the

2. Walter Curt Behrendt, *Modern Building* (New York: Harcourt, Brace & Co., 1937), p. 83.

3. See Alvar Aalto's estimate of the pavilion design in his foreword.

8 FINNISH PAVILION, PARIS EXPOSITION. 1900. "The Finnish Pavilion . . . was, by far, the simplest building at the exposition."

exposition buildings, he was delighted by the companionship of various artists of many countries who met there. During his stay he studied painting under Eugène Carrière, who was then teaching at the Académie Moderne.

In October 1900, Saarinen and his associates were to be presented the medal of the Legion d'Honneur, but the Russian government, for its own reasons, would not permit this award to be presented to the Finnish architects. In an article for *Le Temps*, Anatole France commented favorably on the pavilion's design, remarking on its comparatively simple and forthright quality.

The experience in Paris served to crystallize in Saarinen's mind the nature of the problem of contemporary architecture. "When the future art historian puts the events of present-day art development into writing, he is going to mark the change from the nineteenth century into the twentieth century as that milestone between tradition-bound conservatism and pioneering progressivism," he predicted.

"Naturally, this change has been a slow and gradual one and required a long period of time to become crystallized into its final characteristics. But we are so far advanced into the twentieth century as to make this statement fully justified," he said in 1947.

"Another point to remember in this connection is the fact that the change was very differently timed in the various art forms in various countries. For example, in France, while the impressionist painters protested against the dictatorial rules of the Grand Salon as early as a quarter of a century before the milestone was passed, the chains of the Beaux-Arts architectural style concepts were thrown off as late as a quarter of a century past the time of the passing of the same milestone in the Paris Fair of 1925.

"This is a rather long interval of half a century. But, after all, the milestone is the significant pivot."

4

In their search for expressive form, Eliel Saarinen and his associates in 1900 began with an examination of the importance of material.

"My colleagues and I, in Finland, adhered to the theory that function and material decide the nature of form. This was by no means an original thought; rather, it was a fundamental one. But because this fundamental thought had for so long been buried beneath all kinds of accumulated stylistic nonsense, it was necessary to dig it out from its ornamental grave and to reinstate it in its place of honesty. To do this, however, meant that one had to go backward in time to a period when the employment of material was honest. Such a step was essential to gain the needed knowledge," said Saarinen.

The difficulty of taking this step back into history was that it brought the designers into the realm of romanticism. In the struggle with material, consequently, the young Finnish architects did flounder, now and then, in a morass of "old-time" derivations.

So they faced the problems of a proper use of material, of designing for function with economy. There was nothing to do but to try honestly to take into consideration the basic concepts they were learning with each job.

With these general aims, the young associates designed and constructed a suitable home and studio for themselves. They had need of privacy, for, in their offices in Helsingfors, they had frequent visitors who liked to spend a day in genial conversation. The three decided, then, that they could best accomplish their work if they were to settle outside the city.

On the crest of a hill above the waters of Hvitträsk, "White Lake," about eighteen miles from Helsingfors, the partners found a strikingly beautiful area for their proposed building. In

9 THE SITE OF HVITTRÄSK. "On the crest of a hill above the waters of Hvitträsk—'White Lake'—about eighteen miles from Helsingfors . . ." *Photo by Alfred Nybom.*

10 HVITTRÄSK. COURTYARD VIEW. STUDIO HOME. ". . . pine timbers and granite . . ." *Photo by Loja Saarinen*

the fall of 1901 they purchased a rectangular plot of land on the bluff which bounded the eastern side of the lake. With youthful daring and little money the architects drew up plans that disregarded all stingy limitations. Because of their audacity, Hvitträsk still has incomparable charm.

"On the strength of the jobs we had in view, we approached this project without question, though we were in debt because of it for a long time," said Saarinen as he looked back upon the venture.

During the year 1902 the designs were developed and the building begun. The natural materials at hand—pine timbers and granite—were employed throughout, relieved by passages of glazed brick in certain interior features, such as the fireplaces.

The floor plan of the studio-home received its basic character from the setting. The site of the building sloped down gradually to the north and west. During the winter of 1902, with only the servant quarters and stables constructed, Saarinen lived in the completed section of the structure to supervise the work on that part of the building which was to become the architectural studio and the living quarters of Gesellius, Lindgren, and Saarinen.

The general aspect of the design was, as Saarinen said, romantic. It was, however, not a romanticism deliberately and sentimentally cultivated. It became, purely and honestly, quite naturally, a product of the fundamental nature of the material which was used, fused with the location of the building in a setting of primeval beauty.

"Hvitträsk," the lake's name, which the architects adopted for their dwelling place, was de-

signed to fit the exterior of the building into happy relationship with the environment. The three aspects revealed to the eye of the approaching visitor—the foundation line of rough stone, the relief and contrast of wooden timbers, and the high-pitched roof of red tile—were in harmony with their setting of fir, birch, and pine trees.

"Because we lived here, my associates and I were able, I think, to enter into a deeper contemplation of the basic nature of our work," he said. The serenity of the view from the tower of Hvitträsk, the quiet of the rich forest, and the comfort the designers found in the interiors of their home and workshop kept them on their jobs. "The risk paid off," Saarinen was pleased

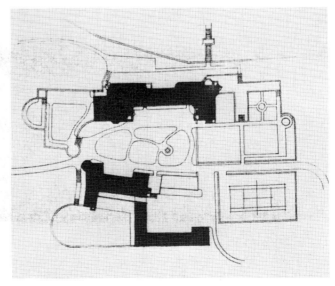

11 HVITTRÄSK. SITE PLAN. ". . . received its basic character from the setting"

13

12 HVITTRÄSK. PENCIL RENDERING OF NORTH ELEVATION FACING THE LAKE. "With youthful daring and little money the architects drew up plans . . ."

to recall. "It proved to be good business and it gave us great pleasure."

Because Saarinen had begun his work in the architectural office by designing furniture, he also took on the task of designing the interiors of the studio-house. That he was thoroughly familiar with the possibilities of personal and useful designs of furniture can be seen in the Hvitträsk interiors.

The structure on the high elevation to the west of Helsingfors has provided material for a number of chapters on the subject of design in architecture, furniture, and other objects of art. In 1905, in *Die neue Rundschau*, Meier-Graefe wrote that "Finland has developed her own art

of building and this art, I think, is the finest fruit of her land . . . it is the product of her own red-blooded youth. Of these I shall name only the three outstanding: Saarinen, Gesellius, and Lindgren. Immediately upon graduation from architectural school these three young men organized a firm in which [each of them] has found an outlet for his particular talents.

"The first named is the strongest creator, an artist of sparkling gifts, who is as familiar with his instinctive knowledge of the nature of materials as the painter with his pigments. Gesellius is the practical mind who performs brilliantly in his profession. Lindgren combines a high creative ability with a fine historical sense. He knows

14

more than anyone else in the country about the medieval Finnish architecture and, what is more important, he knows how to take advantage of this knowledge."[4]

The most complete and the best expression of Eliel Saarinen, up to this point, is to be found in Hvitträsk, the studio-home in which, during the next two decades, he was to work and grow, improve his skill, found a home, and establish his family.

5

Loja Gesellius, the younger sister of Eliel Saarinen's school companion and associate, shared

4. J. Meier-Graefe, "Die Kultur Finnlands," *Die neue Rundschau,* April, 1905, pp. 496–98.

with her brother the advantages of a prosperous, cultivated home. Their father, Hermann Otto Gesellius, a fairly well-to-do importer, gave his children every opportunity to develop. At an early age Loja indicated a strong predilection for the arts, and at the age of twenty-three she went to Paris to study sculpture under Injalbert. She had already shown considerable talent in the Konstföreningen, an art school in Helsingfors. With professional ambition she took advantage of her training period in the studio of the French sculptor.

"All our plans may alter, though," Loja said with no regret, thinking of this early ambition, "and I am not certain anyhow that my opportunities would have made a sculptor of me." Although she did not continue in sculpture, she

13 HVITTRÄSK. NORTH ELEVATION. ". . . foundation of rough stone . . ." *Photo by Loja Saarinen*

14 HVITTRÄSK. BIG GABLE, COURTYARD. ". . . roof of red tile . . ." *Photo by Loja Saarinen*

16

15   HVITTRÄSK. MAIN HALL. ". . . designs were in harmony . . ." *Photo by Loja Saarinen*

16   HVITTRÄSK. ". . . home and workshop . . ." *Photo by Loja Saarinen*

17 ENTRANCE TOWER. *Photo by Loja Saarinen*

employed her gifts in contributing selflessly to the work of her husband and to her children. In the United States she helped to create an art form in weaving which has had a widespread effect to this day.

In 1903, when she returned from Paris, she joined her brother at Hvitträsk, working in her studio on various commissions for sculpture, decorations for interiors, and photography.

She had frequently met Eliel, who, as her brother's friend, had often been a visitor in her home. She had always thought of him as an ascetic, deeply concerned with the weighty problems of life. There had been an earlier marriage for Eliel, but it lasted only briefly. Although divorce was not a small event in the lives of the couple, nor in the social customs of the time, it, nevertheless, seems not to have affected Saarinen's relationship with his partners, or his development as an architect. Soon after the divorce, his first wife married Herman Gesellius, Eliel's partner and Loja's brother, and on March 6, 1904, Eliel married Loja.

As Loja said, she had discovered that "Eliel

was a quiet and thoughtful person who could be funny, too." They shared similar values in the arts, in philosophy, and in life. It was a marriage that lasted for almost fifty years, until Eliel's death in 1950.

Shortly after their marriage, Eliel and Loja Saarinen traveled in Germany, England, and Scotland, where Saarinen made a study of railroad stations—an architectural and engineering problem of considerable complexity. This was the first of their many annual trips to the various countries of Europe. "We traveled each year for perhaps two or three months," remembered Loja Saarinen. "These tours usually included Sweden, Germany, France, and Italy, and combined specific problems in Eliel's work with the fun of travel."

In the spring of 1905 their first child, Pipsan, was born. With the care for her daughter added to the duties of a large household, Loja Saarinen was unable for the next two years to continue her sculpture. And when, later, she was given some free hours for her own work, Loja devoted them to a new occupation using her sculptor's skills. She made and supervised the construction of the architectural and city-plan models which her husband required; the scope of this job is more to be appreciated when the model for Munksnäs-Haga, for example, is studied. The incredible amount of detailed labor that she expended upon such tasks, together with the hospitality she dispensed in the Saarinen home, revealed her energy and ability.

All the arts found expression in the studio-home near Helsingfors. Eliel played the piano and both he and his wife enjoyed evenings devoted to music; frequent visitors with musical talents made the halls of Hvitträsk resound with song and the haunting harmonies of the music of that northern land.

In 1907, Gustav Mahler, the composer and conductor of the Imperial Opera in Vienna, who in that year conducted a series of concerts in Helsingfors, was a guest in the Saarinen home. On this occasion Axel Gallén-Kallela, the Finnish artist and an intimate friend of the Saarinens, painted the musician's portrait.

The annual trip in the spring and summer of 1907 was especially interesting for Eliel Saarinen. Traveling with his wife in France, Switzerland, Germany, and Austria, after taking his competition plans for the Peace Palace to The

Hague, the architect visited Josef Olbrich, in Darmstadt, and the gifted Peter Behrens, in Düsseldorf, whom he had long admired.

Behrens, the leader of German architecture during this decade, was recognized for his practical solutions to the problems met in factory and industrial constructions. Though he was unable to depart from the heavy decorations of classical origins, he resolved the basic demands for a purposive and logical plan to meet contemporary requirements. "I was most interested, though, in Behrens's interiors and in his furniture designs," said Saarinen. It was in Behrens's atelier that Gropius and Mies van der Rohe worked for some time; the studio in Düsseldorf became a potent influence.

Eliel Saarinen's career in this period, marked by intermittent travel, was the time when he responded to the Continental and English-Scottish trend of vanguard design. "I work first and

analyze afterward," he said, "but, of course, the subtle influences of relationship do not preclude the possibility of new thoughts related to new experiences."

In studying contemporary trends, Eliel Saarinen was made more and more aware of the direction in which he himself would go. The trips to various European centers at this stage of his development benefited him.

From far and wide came visitors, too, to the Saarinen home in Finland. The doors of Hvitträsk were open to artists from all parts of the Continent. In 1909, a huge gathering of Scandinavian architects brought a hundred and fifty guests to the Saarinen home, where Loja and Mathilda Gesellius entertained them at a dinner given in the surrounding spacious garden.

"I must confess my sin against my colleagues when, as host to the visiting architects, I found about forty of them ensconced in a temporary

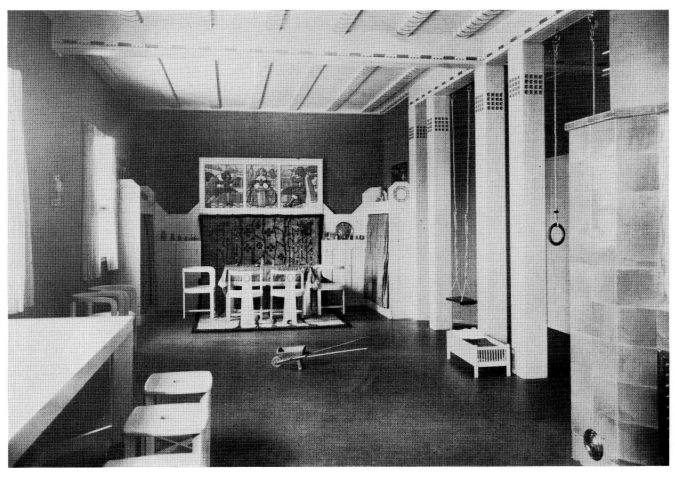

18 HVITTRÄSK. NURSERY. ". . . of advanced trends in design . . ." *Photo by Loja Saarinen*

innocent pleasure." There was some confusion when the architects awoke from their heavy sleep, in a hurry to dress and catch their train to Hvitträsk. Their host had departed on an earlier one.

On August 20, 1910, the second child, a son, was born on Eliel's birthday. He was named Eero, the Finnish form of Eric. A quiet, healthy child, the boy shared with his sister Pipsan the happiness of growing up amid the creative projects with which the studio-home was always filled. They came to accept as a matter of fact the professional problems which were the daily concern of their parents and the associates who worked at Hvitträsk. The children assumed the obligations and joys of their own work as naturally as they engaged in all of the interesting and stimulating activities around them. It was natural then, that Pipsan and Eero made drawings, painted, and modeled from the time they were able to play.

Their early conditioning, which acquainted them with professionalism, unmistakably shaped their later lives. Actually they began their life-work when they were still in childhood. Both Eero and Pipsan continued to work in architecture, sculpture, painting, furniture design, and weaving and accumulated remarkable experience within a few years.

Pipsan, a pretty and vivacious girl, learned readily and became a versatile designer; today she is an interior architect of distinction. She has executed many designs for furniture, glass, rugs, and textiles.

Eero, whose genius was patiently guided by his father and mother, was able before he reached early teens to draw freehand and draft. "I learned while crawling around under my father's drafting table," he used to say. Left-handed, he drew with amazing facility; he was also an excellent watercolorist. At one time his ambition was to become a sculptor.

A mature child for his age, Eero was influenced by the many famed people of great accomplishment whom he had observed at Hvitträsk for as far back as he could remember.

When Julius Meier-Graefe was working on his book about Cézanne, he was a house guest at Hvitträsk for an extended time. A genial companion, he shared honors evenly at the billiard table with Eliel Saarinen. His friendship was one of the happiest that the Geselliuses and Saarinens

SAARINEN SKETCHES. "Frequent visitors with musical talents made the halls of Hvitträsk resound"

dormitory, a part of the hotel dining room in Åbo." said Saarinen. "They were sleeping so peacefully the morning after a festive banquet that I could not resist doing what I did. With tidy care I placed one shoe here, another there, in new arrangements, and mixed up quite a few articles of clothing with a certain amount of enjoyed during their years together. From Florence came Ugo Ojetti, the erudite art critic of the *Corriera della sera;* and from Budapest, the sculptor Géza Maróti, an intimate friend of the family, who frequently enlivened the discussions at Hvitträsk.

In 1905 Eliel Saarinen visited Maxim Gorki in his Finnish country home at Kuokkala. The Russian author, five years Saarinen's senior, became a good friend of the architect. Gorki, whose great tale *Chelkash* won wide attention when Eliel Saarinen was a student of painting in the university art school, was already a veteran revolutionary when they met. He was one of the strongest advocates of liberalism and was frequently sought by the police for his political activities. During one dramatic visit to Hvitträsk, Gorki vanished, escaping the czarist officers who lay in wait for him, and fled to Italy.

"Gorki was a fascinating and many-sided character," said Saarinen. "I remember him most vividly as he was standing in the tower balcony of Hvitträsk one brilliant summer night; throwing up his great, long arms toward the starlit heavens, he exclaimed as he stared out at the dark blue-green hills lighted by an unearthly glow of colored light, 'And there are men who say there is no God!' What do you make of that, when you think of Gorki today? To me he seemed to be a cultivated man, a true humanitarian with a profound love of freedom."

Gallén-Kallela, the Finnish painter, was a constant visitor who enriched the circle at Hvitträsk. An active and loquacious person, he often kept the Saarinens up until daybreak with his wit and charm.

"One morning, at three, I answered the door and received a telegram from Paris from this artist friend. It said, 'Eliel, Eliel, the Lord calls you,' and so I knew that the party in Paris was still well under way," Saarinen recalled of this old friend and his spontaneous ways.

At Stockholm, attending the Olympiad in 1912, the architect and his wife met Carl and Olga Milles. Guests at the home of an old Swedish friend, Saarinen and Milles decided, as the evening's celebration got under way, that they could improve upon some interior arrangements of the house. They agreed upon a plan. During the night they met stealthily and, after hours of desperate, quiet labor, they had changed the din-

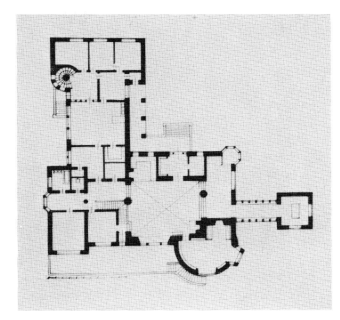

19 SUUR-MERIJOKI. FLOOR PLAN. ". . . an informal arrangement suited to the ground formation"

ing room into the living room and vice versa, complete with pictures, draperies, and rugs. "We must have had some good reason for this—at the time," Saarinen smiled.

"Carl Milles had a beard when I first saw him, so he did not look much like the man we know today. Frank Lloyd Wright would hardly have complained at that time that Milles resembles George Washington more than he does."

Jean Sibelius was thirty-five when he met the artists of Helsingfors at the turn of the century and, when Hvitträsk was built, he and his wife often visited there. Continuing over fifty years, the relationship between the Saarinens and Jean and Aino Sibelius remained loyal and firm. During the war years frequent letters kept them in touch with one another.

Words from a letter just received from the Sibeliuses which Loja was reading to her husband on July 1, 1950, in their bedroom at Cranbrook as he sat in Eero's "womb" chair, were the last he heard. Sibelius wrote, "many hearty thanks for the cigars. When I smoke them the memories of the sparkling parties in Hvitträsk, which Aino and I so thoroughly enjoyed, come back in strong colors." When Loja had finished reading, she turned to Eliel, for he had not answered. His face was serene.

21

20 SUUR-MERIJOKI. EXTERIOR ". . . effect is picturesque . . ." *Etching by Eliel Saarinen*

21 SUUR-MERIJOKI. MAIN ENTRANCE. Watercolor. ". . . a Nordic feeling . . ."

22 SUUR-MERIJOKI. CENTRAL HALL. ". . . furnishings designed and constructed . . ." *Photo by Apollo*

23   SUUR-MERIJOKI. CENTRAL HALL. ". . . harmonious and simply designed furniture." *Photo by Apollo*

6

In 1902, Eliel Saarinen and his associates began to work in their new studios upon an interesting and elaborate plan for Suur-Merijoki, a country estate near Viborg, in eastern Finland. This villa, erected in the same year, was furnished with harmonious and simply designed furniture.

The plan of Suur-Merijoki, as shown in the drawing, was an informal arrangement suited to the ground formation. Designed with no cost limits, it contains generous-sized rooms, curved wall constructions, and lavish living quarters.

The etching of the front elevation shows a pleasantly simple building, with stone foundation, well-placed windows, and a sharply pitched roof. Again, as in the case at Hvitträsk, without

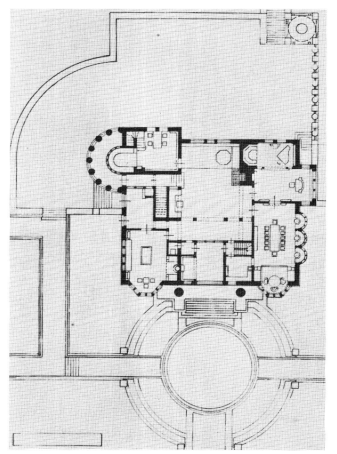

24 MOLCHOW-HAUS. FLOOR PLAN. ". . . was situated on a flat terrain . . ."

a conscious search for a romantic feeling, the effect is picturesque.

Noteworthy in this project is the effort that Eliel Saarinen and his colleagues expended upon the interiors, upon the designs of the doors, fireplaces, wall panels, and hardware. Window draperies, rugs, and upholstery materials were specially designed and woven. Here is a Nordic feeling, stemming from the designers' sympathetic response to the environment.

An interesting contrast may be made here between the concepts of practicality which prevailed in domestic construction at the turn of the century and our contemporary ideas about the number of closets, the placement and completeness of bathrooms, the efficiency of kitchens, the planned and highly designed quality of built-in furniture, as we visualize such conveniences now.

"Fixtures for bathrooms could be readily obtained at this time," said Eliel Saarinen, "though our installation of this equipment had very little in common with the way we manage these things so efficiently today."

So in the Suur-Merijoki country home the floor arrangement presents an interesting study for the woman of today who has just laid aside the latest issue of an architectural magazine filled with laborsaving arrangements in kitchen, bathroom, and closet spaces. The steps forward that have brought the work areas of domestic architecture, for example, into such a prominent position in the consideration of today's builder are immensely satisfying to the housewife. Even the modest cottage has conveniences not known in the most elegant villas of a half-century ago.

The excellence of the country home designed by Eliel Saarinen and his associates cannot, of course, be considered in the light of such contemporary conveniences as today's kitchen. It was not a problem, either, that they were forced to meet; the client was wealthy, servants were obtainable, and the function of the interior was to give refined and comfortable service to the inhabitants. This function the design fulfilled with elegance.

Prevailing in Finland at the turn of the century, as in all parts of Europe and the United States, was the dark, overstuffed, opulently decorated furniture which suggested discomfort and a sense of weird disorder to the generations of a later time. These interiors of Eliel Saarinen are to be judged in contrast. The people of the late nineteenth and early twentieth centuries were not aware of any discomfort. Enthusiastically they darkened the varnishes and brought an ornamental heaviness into their dwelling places.

When the prevailing fashion is kept in mind, the appearance of the light and practical chairs of Suur-Merijoki may be appreciated. They have a clean, clear quality of line that brightens the appearance of the whole room, a comfortable logic in arrangement which is pleasantly inviting. The weighty bulk of the lounge chair of that time is not present in the creation of the Finnish designer.

All the furnishings of this country place had to be constructed under the supervision of the architects. "It was just as much a part of the job to see that the furniture was well done as it was to oversee the construction of the building itself," Saarinen said.

The degree to which Eliel Saarinen was to change and develop his ideas in design is exemplified by a plan completed about five years later for Dr. Paul Remer's house in Germany. Eliel Saarinen was associated at this time with his brother-in-law, Herman Gesellius. Since Armas Lindgren had withdrawn from the firm early in 1905, having been elected head of the school of architecture in Helsingfors, Saarinen and Gesellius worked together on this project. After rejecting many architects of his own country, their German client approached the two associates because he had seen their work in publication and was deeply impressed by it.

"We had the opportunity of working with a very fine fellow," said the architect, "and he was, in many ways, the ideal client. The design included plans for the complete interior, a wonderful chance for Gesellius and me.

"In looking back, one can see that the problems we faced in a time of confused design have to be analyzed beneath their surface, so to speak, in order to discover some of the conflicts that caused the strange divergences and the uncertainty.

"It must be kept in mind, first of all, that, for a long course of four centuries, architectural practice had been a sort of jigsaw puzzle affair, where things were put together in so-called 'composition.' This period of the high and late Renaissance conditioned the architect so that he

became addicted to the belief that this putting together was necessary to produce an art form, subject to the approval of the doctrines of 'established forms.' In following such misleading concepts there was no need, in the mind of the misguided architect, to get down to fundamental principles.

"Two points must be emphasized which contributed to the conflict and confusion. First, the style dictatorship created false security in the minds of the designers, and, second, as a result of this blocked state of mind there was no search for fundamental principles.

"Most urgently something had to be done to build an art form out of the eternal fundamental principles and to bring architecture and design, in general, out of its humiliating state. In order to achieve this goal, it was necessary to free design from its style grip and to let it develop in full freedom according to the nature and character of the time.

"Now a step forward is easy to take, but it became more and more apparent, as we progressed, that there was nothing to substitute for style, nor were there any deep principles discovered by which we might proceed with confidence.

"Some of the results were bound to be unfortunate. One has only to look into the architectural magazines from the dawning years of the new century—particularly into those of France and Germany—to find that things were heading into an alarming form chaos.

25 MOLCHOW-HAUS. MAIN ENTRANCE. ". . . orderly and dignified unity . . . formal gardens, planned to complement the architecture." *Photo by F.K.*

26 MOLCHOW-HAUS. CENTRAL HALL. ". . . light and generous space . . . array of textures . . . furniture created to harmonize with the whole . . ." *Photo by F.K.*

"Thus, in the search for form there was a fight which we had to wage on two fronts: we had to defeat both the spurious character of the stylist and the general debased taste which threatened the formation of true form concepts. In the midst of this fight I learned that my head and heart had to be kept clear so that I could discern between the style-bound and restrained designs and, on the other hand, the debased and undesirable."

A complex situation confronted Eliel Saarinen and his contemporaries. The debasement of public taste in the Western world had its roots, doubtless, in confusion. This confusion resulted from a false idealism, which grew from a misinterpretation of freedom, an uncritical optimism, which stemmed from a misunderstanding of the rights of the individual. It resulted in aesthetic anarchy.

A part of the confusion, however, was the inevitable result of vast materialistic expansion, aided by an unprecedented growth of machine power. This development, seen by many men of goodwill as the beginning of an era of golden prosperity, increased the tempo of the drive toward a general and widespread "improvement" of life.

Factories poured out goods; natural resources fed the greedy manufacturing centers; fabulous sums of money passed among those who controlled these machines and their products. The era from 1860 to the end of the century was "progressive." Unsteady idealism prevailed. Invention of all types was welcomed. Eclecticism, in its unhappiest complexion, was the new aesthetic.

This situation produced the results which may be seen early displayed at the Crystal Palace Exposition in London and late in the International Exposition at Paris. From such eclecticism came architectural confusion, for the jumble of idealism brought forth the addled forms of revivalism, the neglect of function, and the denial of common sense.

"Hence the ill-ventilated, ill-lighted mills, the showy but inconvenient public buildings, the pathetically cheap and crowded schools, the rows of back-to-back houses sitting dank and grim in factory smoke; the public houses, gay with bright lights and bright tile, but innocent of any real beauty; the country houses, aping the castles of medieval nobility or villas of Florence or Rome; the cardboard churches in classic or Gothic or any other style, built like cheap dolls' houses to have an 'effect.' "[5]

5. Talbot Hamlin, *Architecture through the Ages* (New York: G. P. Putnam's Sons, 1940), p. 542.

Such scenes are what Eliel Saarinen saw when he looked about him, and such architecture is what he alluded to when he spoke of the debased and undesirable.

"Then I learned, also, that even when the struggle was honest and sincere, it was still possible to violate the clearest primary principles because these principles were not clearly apprehended. But as the search progressed and the struggle went on, some leading thoughts sprang up which pointed a direction. These thoughts were manifold in variety and born of different points of view. But some of them were fundamental principles.

27 MOLCHOW-HAUS. SKETCHES. "In the sketches the progressive stages of visualization are revealed"

28 MOLCHOW-HAUS. SKETCH OF INTERIOR. ". . . marked the quality of the draftsmanship"

"First among these, as I pointed out, came the problem of material," said Eliel Saarinen. "And yet, when a sound and logical idea of material use was issued, it was often vitiated through the interference of style.

"So then came the problem of function, which, because it is fundamentally inherent in all things, should not have given the slightest reason for separate consideration. Yet, because of the curse of style domination, there was a need for an awakening influence to bring function into its proper and logical place. When function had been properly stressed—and Louis Sullivan's noble statement was only an expression of the advanced spirit of the time—it became the keystone to organic building.

"But then, as I pointed out before, came a recurring threat of style, this time in the guise not of the repetition of classical formalisms but of the new organic 'ism.'"

Eliel Saarinen had to work his way out of this confusion, as did his colleagues, who sought seriously the basic principles of design. The Remer commission offered the opportunity to advance; the solutions to this problem are honest, logical, and tasteful.

Beginning the design for this country estate, to be erected in Mark Brandenburg in 1905, Saarinen and Gesellius completed the project within two years. Because this structure was erected in Germany, it was flavored, in keeping with Eliel Saarinen's sympathy with the individual location of each design that he created, with the spirit of central Europe.

Molchow-Haus, as this country place was named, was situated on a flat terrain. The floor plan shows how the designer recognized this situation by executing a form of orderly and dignified unity, less informal than the plan of a forest-bound structure in a mountainous country site would have been. Surrounding the building is an impressive arrangement of formal gardens, planned to complement the architecture.

Of particular interest, however, is the clean, unhampered line of the interior. There, skillfully combined, are the quietly refined rooms, with light and generous space enriched by a thoughtful array of textures, and the simple furniture created to harmonize with the whole.

These interiors for Molchow-Haus show clearly to what extent Eliel Saarinen and his associates had developed in the vanguard of progressive European thought since they had drawn the designs for Suur-Merijoki in 1902. In the German house the elements of romanticism, indicated by a generous use of curved-line elements, were largely eliminated. The fight for logic and clear simplicity, which is the best of the honesty of Eliel Saarinen, was furthered, and the front was widened, in this building at Brandenburg. But the deeper significance of this change is indicated by the more comprehensive manner in which the designer solved his basic problems of material and function.

The material out of which Dr. Remer's house was fashioned was one which suggested a formal

29 MOLCHOW-HAUS. KITCHEN. ". . . a light, sanitary, and spacious workroom . . ." *Photo by F.K.*

30 HELSINGFORS RAILROAD STATION. SITE PLAN. ". . . complex problems of architecture and society"

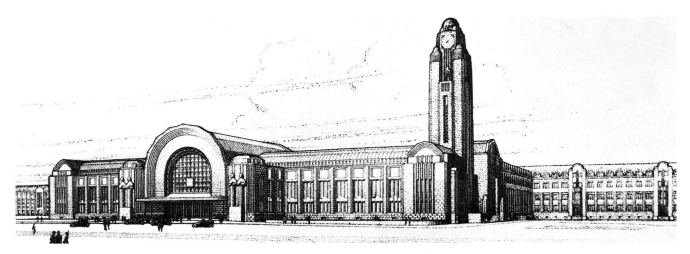

31 HELSINGFORS RAILROAD STATION. FRONT ELEVATION. ". . . beginning with ancient principles . . ."

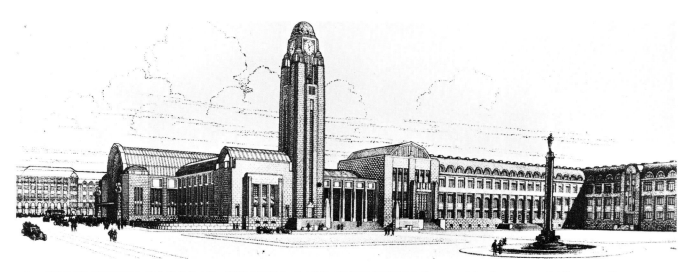

32 HELSINGFORS RAILROAD STATION. EAST ELEVATION. ". . . end in the personal idiom . . ."

33 HELSINGFORS RAILROAD STATION. WEST ELEVATION. SOUTHWEST CORNER. "... that kind of architectural thinking which designed the great monuments of high civilizations ..." *Photo by Eric Sundström*

34 HELSINGFORS RAILROAD STATION. MAIN ENTRANCE. "... unity in form ..." *Photo by Eric Sundström*

35 HELSINGFORS RAILROAD STATION. PART OF MAIN FAÇADE. "The architect's concern for tower construction . . ." *Photo by Eric Sundström*

treatment. The designer moved toward the simplicity which the stucco invited. That clean, thin quality was transferred with logic into the nature of the interior and the furniture. The point must be stressed that, as this example shows, Eliel Saarinen did not preconceive his solutions in the light of an *idée fixe*. The example does reveal, however, that he was creating form as a mature personality who expressed himself in a personal way.

The Brandenburg building is the result of a healthy development, conscious of its qualities and purposes, in almost instinctive harmony with the best trend of the time and endowed with the specific character of the designer.

One of the most satisfying areas of this design was developed in the kitchen—a light, sanitary, and spacious workroom that presaged the important place in domestic architecture which that room has attained in subsequent decades. This kitchen has a remarkably modern feeling.

In the sketches the progressive stages of visualization are revealed. The ability Saarinen had manifested as a student of painting has always marked the quality of his draftsmanship.

7

It was not until Eliel Saarinen began his work on the competition for the railroad station at Helsingfors, his first expression in the monumental, that he was introduced to the more complex problems of architecture in its relation to society.[6] In 1899 he and his associates had given thought to city planning, but in an abstract way; the ideas of many progressive designers were directed toward community improvement. In 1904 Saarinen came face to face with numerous conflicting forces, diverse and confused, which can easily defeat the best-laid plans of architects.

During the expansion of industrial power in the Western world, the railroad station, symbol of the huge financial force behind it, had grown to gigantic proportions. Little, if any, common sense had been used in its design. Earlier in the nineteenth century the terminals of the English railroads, for example, had been forthright and honest reception centers for the traveler and his baggage. The tycoon who spread the rail patterns over the length and breadth of the land, however, was not content to have a simple, direct solution to the problem of receiving this traffic; he had to build a monument to himself, usually in the form of a Roman bath.

While Latrobe and Mills in the United States and Friedrich Schinkel in Germany had set a salutary example in the construction of practical buildings, later reckless developments and the wealth of the railroads fostered an unfortunate vitiation of the purity of these builders. When Eliel Saarinen began his sketches for the Helsingfors station, the confusion of designs had brought about a deplorable state of affairs in all countries where industry had expanded the rail systems and where the huge ugly terminals had been accepted.

The planning of a railroad passenger terminal was a problem of enormous complexity exceeded only by that of a modern airport, as his son Eero discovered when he designed the Dulles Airport in Washington, D.C., forty years later. Little is determined that enables the designer to proceed even into first concepts. The matter of site may

6. See Carroll L. V. Meeks, *The Railroad Station: An Architectural History* (New Haven: Yale University Press, 1956).

36 HELSINGFORS RAILROAD STATION. DRAWING OF WAITING ROOM. "... Today it is too small ..."

37 HELSINGFORS RAILROAD STATION. MAIN ENTRANCE HALL. "... should be increased ..." *Photo by Eric Sundström*

be open and confused by conflicting economic interest. The city plan, if one exists, must be followed, or it must be changed. Coordination must be brought about between bus, streetcar, and automobile transportation. Grade crossings must be considered and safe solutions presented. Furthermore, the operation of the rail traffic must be thoroughly studied and provision made for later expansion. The scope of the job and the proportion of the principal facilities must be subjected to a consideration of building costs, balanced against the funds available.

While the newspapers, promoting public interest, sympathized with the efforts of the political forces in taking a stand for the rights of the common man, vested interests, concerned with determining noble purposes for certain properties, conflicted with the board of trustees of the railroad organization who had inflexible ideas of its own. As a result, the railroad terminal designer was faced on all fronts by complex and active opposition.

In designing the railroad station for Helsingfors, Saarinen soon discovered the variety and strength of these opposing forces. His first fight with the board of the railroad organization concerned the location of the station; he lost that battle to the officials who rejected his plan.

Next, after he had made a thorough study of the function of the railroad yard, that plan was rejected. Then, in suggesting the size of the building, the designer envisioned the future service of the station in modern times and decided that it should be large enough to accommodate the shops which are, today, a part of every well-conceived terminal. His visionary scheme was overruled—the cost would be too high. Confined within such limitations, the designer produced his scheme for the Finnish railroad station which, in years to come, was to be acclaimed by the architectural world.

The initial phase of the construction, according to the original design of 1904, was carried on between 1905 and 1907. For the investigation which Eliel Saarinen always made in preparation for an important design, he and his wife traveled to England and Scotland where they found no help for his problem. Finally, they went to Frankfurt-am-Main. There some of the functional construction, though hidden in decoration, had been intelligently thought out by J. W.

Schwedler in 1888. In general, however, it appears that, as Alfred Fellheimer points out, "those who have been prominently connected with the design of notable passenger terminals have literally grown up with them through the era of their development."[7] With no comparable industrial experience, Saarinen had to solve his own problem through careful and extensive research.

Depending upon his ingenuity, skill, and vision in creating a plan to satisfy the myriad requirements of the project, he developed the total design in 1910, which has been a monument in the history of modern transportation facilities. The station proper, which was not completed until 1914, required four years to build.

"It is not a satisfactory unit yet," judged Eliel Saarinen. "After the First World War, Finland was too deeply wounded to do more than repair the destruction which the station suffered during the war when it was converted into a Russian military hospital. It is too small, and some features of the practical elements of the transportation service should be reexamined."

American architects saw this design as the beginning of the Finnish designer's fame. It was an eloquent denunciation of all the "classic" nonsense which had been erected at the terminal point of a maze of steel tracks. European designers received some lessons from it, too, and the achievement of Eliel Saarinen was widely acknowledged.

In 1914, shortly after the completion of the Helsingfors station, Karl Ernst Osthaus wrote in a discussion of European railway terminals: "The most beautiful railroad station, however, is neither in Prussia nor in all Germany . . . it is in Helsingfors, the creation of the greatest Finnish architect, Eliel Saarinen."[8] The weight of such praise can be appreciated when the railroad stations at Dresden and Dortmund, designed by August Klönne, are studied in comparison. The progress of steel constructions had gone on apace; the flight of girders had freed the imaginations of many contemporary designers. Numerous good examples of functional quality in excellent design come from the period to which Osthaus refers.

7. Alfred Fellheimer, "Modern Railway Passenger Terminals," *Architectural Forum* 53 (December 1930): 655.

8. "Der Bahnhof," *Der Verkehr: Jahrbuch des Deutschen Werkbundes* (Jena: Eugen Diederichs, 1914), p. 41.

Why, then, was the Finnish railway station acclaimed with such enthusiasm? It is the honesty of the solution of the practical problem which engineers and architects recognized: the freedom from a dead formalism, the intelligent combination of simple mass and suitable sculpture, and, most significantly, the artistry of the designer giving the full measure of his experience and talent to achieve convincing balance.

With his feeling for the monumental, Eliel Saarinen was able to relate the parts of the Helsingfors station to the harmony of the whole. This unity was expressed in a form which, having its beginning in the ancient principles of design, had its end in the personal idiom of the creator.

"Art is either a plagiarist or a revolutionist," Paul Gauguin said. The railway station helped to make clear the issue between the camp of the imitators and that small band of artists who were giving new and appropriate form to the architecture of their time. Eliel Saarinen shunned imitation; he dared assert the need for that kind of architectural thinking which designed the great monuments of high civilizations.

While it is impossible to be absolutely sure what will last, time itself does finally give us a judgment about the quality of any man-made object. The Helsingfors station has been acclaimed by time. It stands today as a monument of honesty and courage, representing the nature of the spirit in which it was created.

In a discussion of Eliel Saarinen's talent for the monumental in design, it is timely at this point in his story, to recall the conception which he began in 1905, a design for the Palace of Peace at The Hague.

The Finnish architect received an invitation, as did twenty-three architects of other nationalities, to participate in an international competition for the palace which was to house the work for peace and good will, a home for the spirit of international cooperation which was thought, in that optimistic moment of history, to be the blessing of the new century.

The great venture was as ill-fated architecturally as it was politically. The judges of the competition, driven by the same motives of compromise which infected the minds of the nationalistic representatives who later worked and failed in that huge structure, turned away from the invitation of tomorrow and looked back to the more dismal aspects of yesterday. In 1907 the award was granted to a feeble, eclectic misconception.

Eliel Saarinen's design stirred up heated dissension among those who arranged the competition. There was a good deal of feeling on the part of some of the members that Saarinen's plans should be adopted. Any breath of progressivism, however, was smothered by the coldly conservative majority of the group. While the monumental plan submitted by Finland's architect was not one of his major accomplishments, it did make a contemporary approach to the problem.

The Hague design is one of the stages through which Eliel Saarinen passed in his evolution toward a more complete realization of the monumental. In itself, he believed, the design made no important contribution to the history of modern architecture.

During the spring and summer of 1907 Eliel and Loja Saarinen traveled through Europe after taking the plans for the Palace of Peace to The Hague. In the following year in his studio at Hvitträsk, he devoted much of his time to the design of Landtdagshuset, the Finnish House of Parliament, for which he eventually received the first prize in a national competition (see frontispiece). Serving on the jury which awarded this coveted honor were Ragnar Östberg, the talented Swedish architect, and Hermann Billing, the German.

Because of the influence of the czarist government, this national symbol of Finnish unity was never built. This is but another frustration in the history of Finland during this century which seemed to promise so much of freedom, equality, and opportunity.

To the Finnish architect's concept of his country's monument Ragnar Östberg paid tribute: "The sense of unity with which Saarinen's project has been accomplished is majestic and by no means common among the work of contemporary architects. And this I say with emphasis: indeed, the simplicity of this design is wonderful to behold as it is presented in all its harmony. And what a powerful conception is needed for the artist to attain this!"[9]

9. Ragnar Östberg, "Finlands Nya Landtdagshus," *Arkitektur* 38 (April 4, 1908): 41–44.

Eliel Saarinen was thirty-five years of age when he designed Landtdagshuset. Having had the good fortune to begin his work in a period of youthful stirring within the soul of his native land, he had progressed rapidly with the demanding times. He had gained, in a brief period, an experience unusual for one of his age.

The challenge of the Landtdagshus competition became one of great significance to the designer for he was capable of seeing the scope of such problems. With increasing knowledge he undertook his succeeding work with confidence.

In this structure, which was to be situated on Observatory Hill, Eliel Saarinen advanced in the personal quality of his design. Bold, straight, and austere as the northland, the drawing reveals the imaginative decoration which warms the detail of this structure. It foreshadows the life-character of the artist.

The parliament building was designed to thrust upward from a commanding site so that it would dominate the view from a great distance. "Though I was impressed, of course, with the significance of this opportunity," said Eliel Saarinen, "I approached the problem altogether with the eye of a designer. For me it was a magnificent architectural opportunity upon which I spent the best thought I had at that time."

In timely coordination with the competition for the national monument of government was the movement of unification in Finland in the year 1905. It was then that the aristocracy officially gave the government of Finland over to total representation, though in reality the Finnish people had been imbued with democratic concepts of government for many years. The step toward total representation in 1905, however, was the final manifestation of the inner working power of democracy in that northland, subject in some degree to the power of the czarist governor in Finland.

Political relations between Russia and Finland were delicate, with constant threats of outbursts on the part of nationalist Finns who were striving valiantly for the complete emancipation of their country. Culturally, the relations between the educated Finn and the Russian were not too bad; social and professional intercourse was widespread. Eliel Saarinen, for example, had many friends in Saint Petersburg—among them, Diaghilev, Grabar, Leonid Andreev, and Roerich—whom he visited on those frequent occa-sions when he traveled to that city to visit his parents who were still in the Lutheran parsonage at Saint Petersburg.

The growing and eager spirit of Finnish self-realization was expressed in the competition for the parliament house. The building was to be the symbol of the nation, physical evidence of the trust with which the Finnish citizen looked to the future of his country.

In strong, simple lines Eliel Saarinen spoke of his nation's hope and faith. Concerned for years with the problem of the vertical climax above the founding horizontal weight, he succeeded in producing one of the impressive designs that have come from his disciplined hand—a symmetrically balanced structure with a strong vertical climax, relieved by tastefully arranged details.

8

From the beginning of Eliel Saarinen's architectural career, ideas about city planning had been studied in the offices where he was associated. The larger concept dealing with congested conditions in concentrated population centers attracted the idealist in Saarinen's makeup. Gradually he had come to see that the limitations of the specialist prevented any solution of the problems of the city; the architect, as the creator of individual, isolated units of habitation, was not going to get at the heart of the matter by turning all his attention to the job before him on his drawing table.

38 LOJA SAARINEN. *Photo by Apollo*

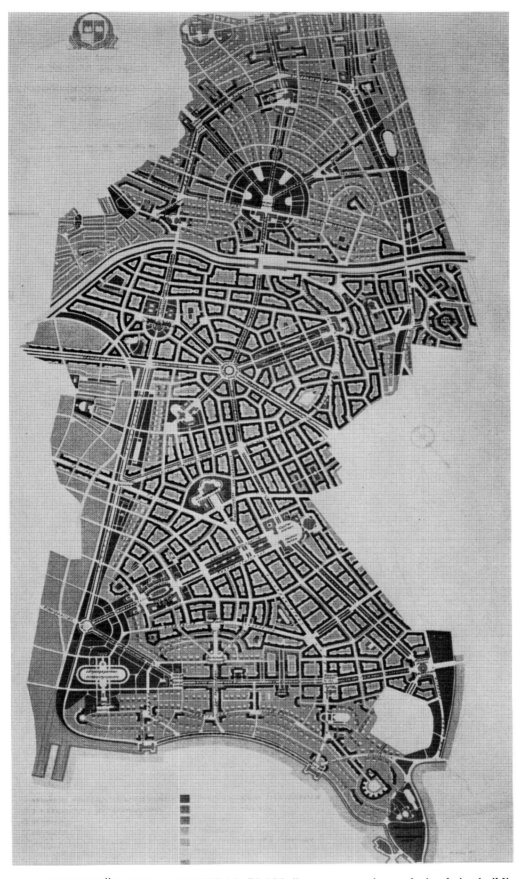

39 MUNKSNÄS-HAGA. GENERAL PLAN. ". . . an extensive analysis of city-building . . ."

The whole philosophy of individualism of the past century was not compatible with the vision of city planning. Only after economic, social, and political forces have been compelled to see that the laissez-faire spirit will not suffice can the far-seeing solutions of city planning receive favorable attention. And because the life force that shapes the city is sinfully neglectful of the fate of the inhabitants, the designer who dreams of real solutions requires the sustaining power of idealism; he must have profound patience and a reservoir of energy to carry him undiscouraged through the long years.

Though the visions of some Renaissance plans were far-flung and the experiments of men like Haussmann must be revered as the work of daring pioneers, the city's difficult task of righting itself belongs to this century. In the congested center the life force—a complex, hydra-headed composition of basic elements having to do with geography, economics, sociology, finance, politics, education, and ignorance—becomes more involved as the problem becomes more pressing. It may be that the hope of the city actually lies in the condition in which it finds itself after haphazard growth; it is so bad that it must be improved. That is where we are today.

Eliel Saarinen and his colleagues were absorbed in this problem. They had the optimism at first of the men like Otto Wagner who looked with expectation toward the progress of industrial growth. This was the final optimism of the Renaissance, the last flush of spiritual prosperity, which was to meet with disillusionment in the First World War.

A practical model in city planning at the turn

41 MUNKSNÄS-HAGA. "A study of the remarkable model . . ." *Model by Loja Saarinen*

of the century was created by Tony Garnier's industrial city, which he designed between 1901 and 1904. Here, for the first time, the contemporary solution to the questions of transportation, recreation, work, and residence was suggested in a way that might be practicable. Yet the efforts of the visionaries who made plans were, by and large, of negligible importance.

"Just at the time when the creative instinct for town-building was most needed," as Eliel Saarinen saw it, "it ceased to exist. The sense for the most comprehensive art of man was lost. Yet the great loss was not understood, much less regretted."

Perhaps the most important impetus toward the salvation of the city came from the expressions of the hopeful who were able to state the problem with clarity and bring to the attention of designers the acuteness of the problem. Among those who contributed a chapter to this expression was Camillo Sitte, a Viennese design-

40 MUNKSNÄS-HAGA. AERIAL VIEW. Drawing

42 MUNKSNÄS-HAGA. DETAIL. ". . . reveals the nature of this design." *Model by Loja Saarinen*

er who published his *Town-Building According to Artistic Principles* in 1889. As Sirén put it, "He opened our eyes to the picturesque, untrammeled beauty of the medieval city." In the preface of Eliel Saarinen's *The City*, Sitte's influence is evident.

The gradual dissatisfaction that came over the cities of the Western world, disorganized and growing at an alarming pace, made fertile ground for the seed which men like Sitte sowed. In a general and philosophical statement of urban confusion, with some suggested solutions to the problem of the city, Sitte arrived at three important conclusions: he saw the importance of informal and pliable town planning; he stressed the need of intelligent coordination of the whole through correlation of units; and he realized the need of forming streets and open spaces into functional spatial enclosures.

"Sitte's influence in northern Europe has been remarkable," said Saarinen. "His message was

fundamental in that it used history to point out the need for meeting the contemporary problem with contemporary methods. His was neither an old nor a modern idea; and it was one with universal and everlasting significance."

Eliel Saarinen, in company with Julius Tallberg and Leo Lerche, two clients who were interested in developing an area near Helsingfors, traveled to Stockholm, Copenhagen, Hamburg, Karlsruhe, and Munich to study a number of private developments and some regional planning which was relatively well advanced, especially in Stockholm and in Copenhagen. "We visited the city-planning offices, when such had been established, and found sympathetic colleagues involved in far-flung problems of planning," he said.

Upon their return to Helsingfors, the architect and his clients signed the contract for the plan of Munksnäs-Haga, a site near the city. The development of this design, in which Saarinen was ably assisted by Loja Saarinen who built all the models, was to take four years. Of course, during this period the architect continued to work on other projects, some of them of considerable importance, such as the City Hall in Lahti, Finland; the city plan for Canberra, the capital of Australia; and the city plan for Reval, Estonia.

The Munksnäs-Haga plan became an extensive analysis of the city-building problem, which Eliel Saarinen completed and published in Helsingfors in August, 1915. In October there was a ceremonious opening of the exhibition of the models, plans, and charts at Riddarhuset in the capital city.

Julius Tallberg, a man of spirit and imagination inspired by the example of a group of architects who had planned a section of Helsingfors for ideal living, purchased a peninsular area near the city. He was interested in creating a profit-producing community in which his firm would sell lots and control the construction. This was the initial step in the development of Tallberg's "Pro Helsingfors," an ideal city beautified by sculpture, architectural decoration, and allied arts.

Eliel Saarinen had known the Finnish businessman since he and his associates first opened an office in 1896, when they won a competition for an apartment house that Tallberg wanted to construct. Since that first meeting the architect had

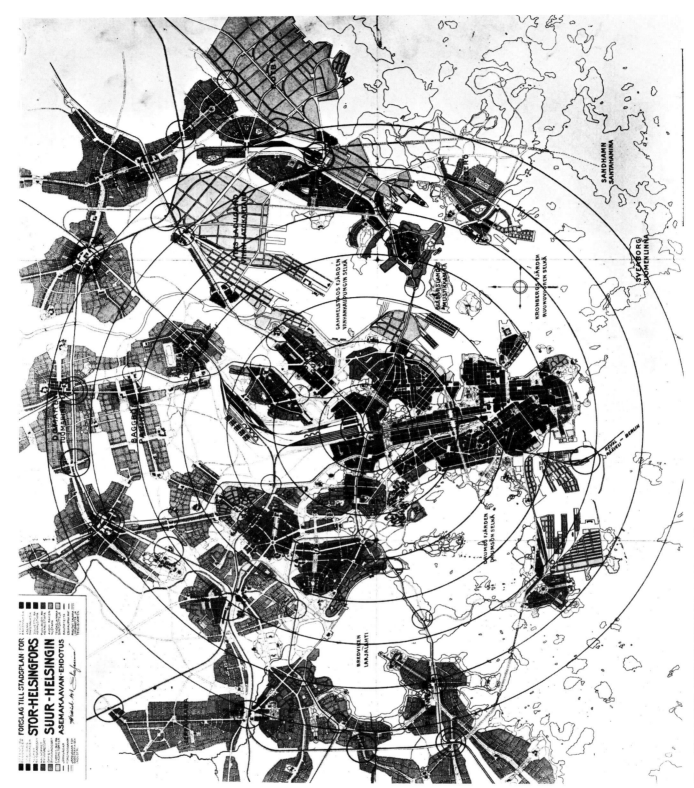

43 GREATER HELSINGFORS. DECENTRALIZATION LAYOUT. "The Munksnäs–Haga plan became an extensive analysis of the city-building problem which Eliel Saarinen completed and published in . . . August, 1915."

44 GREATER HELSINGFORS. CENTRAL SECTION OF DECENTRALIZATION PLAN. Drawing

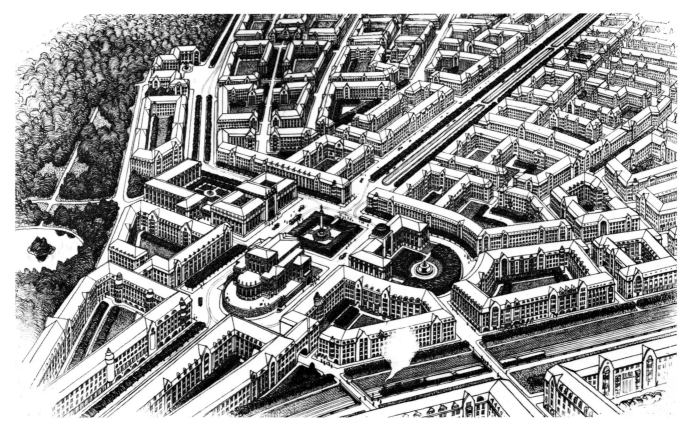

45 REVAL, ESTONIA. AERIAL VIEW. ". . . Reval was a promising place for an impressive harbor development"

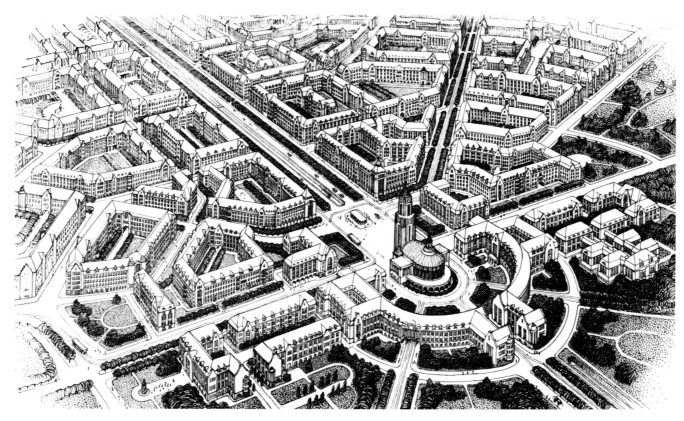

46 REVAL, ESTONIA. AERIAL VIEW. HOSPITAL CENTER IN RESIDENTIAL SECTION

47 REVAL, ESTONIA. AERIAL VIEW. CITY HALL

seen the scope of the financier's operations; the Munksnäs-Haga idea was the most ambitious of them.

The plan for the suburb of Helsingfors was one that set the arrangements of structures in logical, compact, and close areas. A study of the remarkable model Loja Saarinen constructed reveals the nature of this design.

The larger vision, though, was the more important one; it had to do with the total reconstruction of the city of Helsingfors. Here Saarinen expressed, for the first time, the decentralization concept of city building in anticipation of the new modes of transportation and communication which were on the horizon of the future. In carefully conceived units, which provided for the relocation of working and living areas, he created a milestone in the development of city planning.

When Eliel Saarinen had completed the plan, it was published in Helsingfors.[10] In this design the architect initially worked out his principle of architectural order, that is, the fundamental place of design in the total order of life.

With design as the basic consideration, architectural order may be achieved. The plan of the city must be approached with this concern for architectural order—an order which takes into consideration the sociological problem and the physical problem; which stresses the principles of expression, correlation, and organization; and which, finally, seeks its expression in the propitious architectural moment.

The moment will reveal its nature when the

10. Bertel Jung, *Pro Helsingfors* (Helsingfors: Lilius & Hertzberg, 1918).

problem under consideration has been intelligently and thoroughly examined to determine the condition created by the life force. That nature must be reflected in the design.

This idea Eliel Saarinen tried to work out practically in his plan for the greater Helsingfors. His solution has been a source book for students of city building for the last three decades. The efforts he expended upon the problem of the city contributed to the body of knowledge on community planning, the vital need of today's urban centers. Later in his book *The City*[11] he presented the fruit of his studies.

In 1911 Eliel Saarinen was invited to Budapest to advise in the development of that city. As a result of his analysis, he wrote a brochure on the planning problems of Budapest which was published in 1912.

In January, 1911, he became consultant in city planning at Reval, Estonia, and two years later, in April, 1913, he received the first award in an international competition for a plan for that city.

Under Russia, Reval was a promising place for an impressive harbor development. The reason for Saarinen's commission was clearly to develop an outlet, a seaway for Moscow; the future seemed to indicate that Reval would build in a proportion which would insure a monumental gateway for traffic to the West and a door to Russia. The war, however, brushed aside this project, and no part of Saarinen's plan was ever completed.

11. Reissued in August, 1965, in paperback, by the Massachusetts Institute of Technology Press.

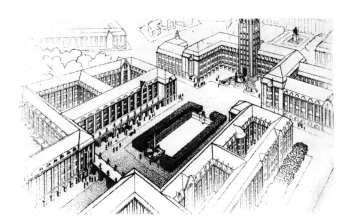

48 REVAL, ESTONIA. CENTRAL CITY HALL COURT. ". . . the architecture, . . . a standard character which only indicates the general disposition of the buildings"

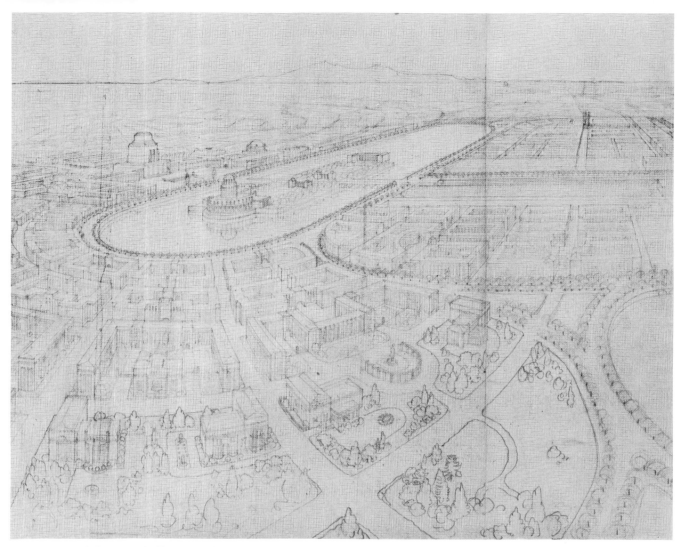

49 CANBERRA, AUSTRALIA. GENERAL LAYOUT OF THE CENTRAL PART OF THE CITY. " 'I learned

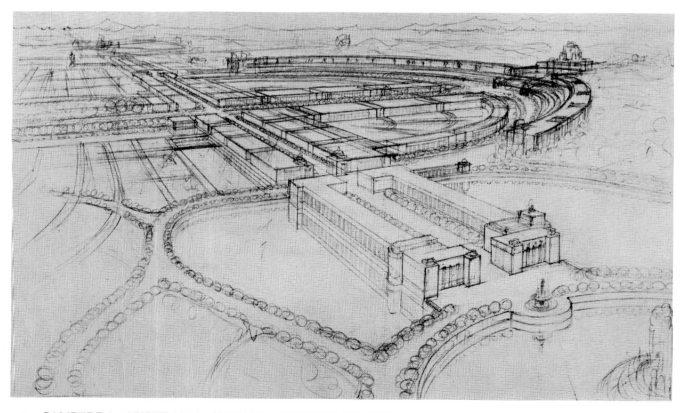

50 CANBERRA, AUSTRALIA. SKETCH. MUSEUM ISLAND

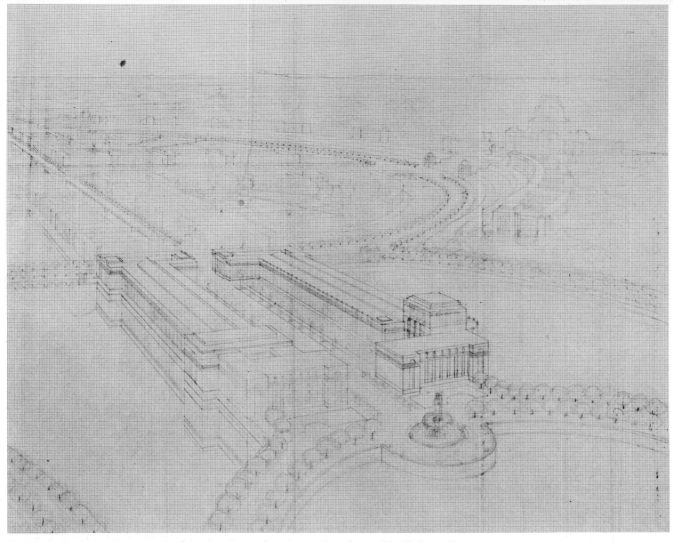

in this competition that the absolute freedom of such a project is too idealistic . . ."

51 CANBERRA, AUSTRALIA. SKETCH. PARLIAMENTARY GROUP

52 CANBERRA, AUSTRALIA. SKETCH. MUSEUM BUILDINGS

In this design the Finnish architect created a formal and orderly radiation from a central, monumental building. The wide highways leading out from this center were bordered by shrubbery and trees. The architecture was conceived in a standard character indicating the general disposition of the buildings, usually in open spaces in the form of courts.

"The purpose of this plan is to create a system of controls, to accommodate expansion, in which

a principle of general development is set forth; a principle which ought gradually to penetrate future growth, so that the city may enjoy a healthy, normal development by anticipating those various problems which can be practically visualized. The modern city plan must solve these problems in a practical, hygienic and aesthetic manner," wrote Eliel Saarinen in 1913.[12]

Not only did the Reval plan aim to serve the needs of the immediate present, it also aspired to show how the citizens of any community might support the construction of a clean and beautiful city.

As Le Corbusier says: "The structure of cities reveals two possibilities: a progressive growth, subject to chance, with resultant characteristics of slow accumulation and gradual rise; once it has acquired its gravitational pull it becomes a centrifugal force of immense power, bringing the rush and the mob. . . . Or on the other hand, the construction of a city may be the expression of a preconceived and predetermined plan embodying the then known principles of the science of planning."[13]

12. "Stadtplanung für Reval," *Der Städtebau*, vol. 18, no. 5/6.

13. Jeanneret-Gris (Le Corbusier), *The City of Tomorrow* (New York: Payson & Clarke, 1929), pp. 91–92.

53 ISLAND IN THE FINNISH GULF. Watercolor. 1900. "As he surveyed the landscape of Finland, the broad pattern of the hillside, sea and valley, he sensed the harmony . . ."

54 EDINBURGH CASTLE. Watercolor. 1904. ". . . In the silhouette of a landscape he comprehended simplicity. This quality he translated . . ."

In the plan for Reval, the Finnish architect expounded the idea that the controlled city design may produce for the benefit of the future a condition which, though it may not be the solution of a particular time and of one designer, would justify forethought. The city planner produces the leaven which leavens the lump; the forgotten schemes of visionary architects have not met with total defeat. Each plan is a step in a gradual process of socioeconomic education.

Along with the plan for Reval, Eliel Saarinen was working on his design for Canberra, the capital of Australia, a plan which received the second prize in 1912 (the first award went to Griffin, of Chicago). At first glance the Canberra project seemed to be a splendid opportunity. A city was to be planned with but few limitations. Upon closer examination, however, the competition proved to be the result of the envious aspirations of Sidney and Melbourne; a compromise between the two cities had been achieved by the selection of Canberra for a capital site. Further, the freedom from realistic limitations proved again that creative forces need an obstacle in order to grow through conquering it.

"I learned," Eliel Saarinen recalled, "in this competition that the absolute freedom of such a project is too idealistic; the imagination does not work soundly when it is free from difficulty. We must strain against limitations."

9

In a study of an artist's work there is always the attempt to create from chaotic detail a coherent structure that shows the large outlines of the trends which the artist's creations reveal. Analysis may often be rewarded with some general and orderly arrangements, but there seems to be no way of indicating the whole process of an artist's self-discovery. Human personality is too subtle and complex to permit dissection. The mind of an artist is not subject to tests and measurements.

The artist's experiences can partly explain his work, of course. The facts about Eliel Saarinen's life will not reveal all he was; they can only suggest how he became what he was. This record of the events of his life, in showing some of the strong influences that played upon the man, however, offers a degree of understanding of the nature of the designer.

"The mistake in all modern psychological biography," says Otto Rank in his penetrating work, *Art and Artist*, "lies in its attempt to 'explain' the artist's work by his experience, whereas creation can only be made understandable through the inner dynamism and its central problems."[14]

14. Otto Rank, *Art and Artist* (New York: Alfred A. Knopf, 1932), p. 49.

55 PONT NEUF. PARIS. Sketch. 1912. ". . . into paintings which contained both the natural and man-made forms; he blended the shapes of hills with those of houses. Harmony resulted"

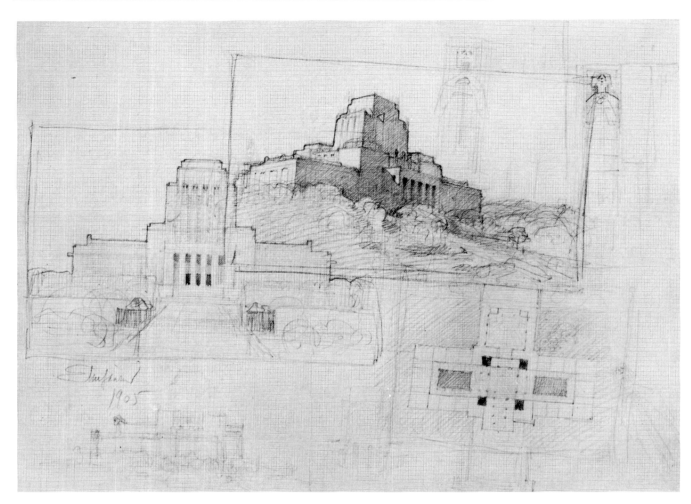

56 FINNISH PARLIAMENT HOUSE. SKETCHES. ". . . transition between natural forms and the man-made forms"

It is significant, though, that when Sigfried Giedion says, "History is not a compilation of facts, but an insight into a moving process of life," he adds that certain specific events must be examined minutely so that a culture may be seen from within as well as from without.[15] Because men make history, Giedion's thought may encompass biography as well. While a chronology will contain the facts of an artist's life, only a contemplative examination of these facts will obtain an insight into the moving process of that life. The factual material presents an opportunity, perhaps the sole tangible one, to see within.

The temperament of the artist—the inner dynamism, the constitutional endowment, the genius—finds expression in varied and original ways. One will reveal his predilection for thin shape,

for a high intensity of color, for a slender volume or a curved form; another is predisposed to a heavy space, a low tone, full volume, and linear constructions of infinite tension. These differences in expression make the variety that enriches the arts.

Because a man's work becomes the all-important reflection of his personality, a careful look at it reveals the qualities of the man himself. When an artist's work is considered in the light of the information that surrounds him, the personality stands forth, unanalyzed but clear, to the imaginative mind. Although neither the personality nor the work it created is explained by these facts of experience, these facts do lead to a partial understanding of the "inner dynamism" and its central problem.

In this account of the facts about Eliel Saarinen, one characteristic which can be noted and expanded with illustrations from his work

15. Sigfried Giedion, *Space, Time, and Architecture* (Cambridge: Harvard University Press, 1941), p. iv.

is his love of nature; it is significant that he studied it with the eyes of a painter. Like a number of architects—like Le Corbusier, for example—who have contributed to the history of contemporary design, he was a painter, first, who turned to architectural design after he had been trained in the skills and techniques of painting.

A basic lesson in painting is that the given shape upon which the artist works must receive first consideration. In the painter's studio this approach means that the artist must bend his initial concentration to the problem of totality; he must consider the significance of the whole. The painter attacks the given shape, laying in the large areas, modeling and remodeling the larger aspects of his idea with no regard for detail. When he has satisfied his own critical demands, he begins to give thought to the content of the various areas of shape.

The painter, working with line, shape, value, color, and texture, gains experience with the possibilities of these qualities; he learns to study nature with these elements in mind. The shape of a branch, the form of a rock, the light and dark patterns in a field, the hue of a brick wall and its peculiar pattern, are impressed upon his mind. As he becomes sensitive to these qualities in nature, he transfers his feelings to his canvas. It becomes, then, one might say, a controlled and controllable experience. In the development of the easel picture the artist works with the areas indicated and aims, ultimately, in all the aspects of his craft, to satisfy his conscience. He must continue to work until he has fulfilled the demand that he makes upon himself.

The demand of the artist comes from within. It defines the character of the artist; he must be possessed of an ideal, and he must be imaginative

57   A TOWER SKETCH. Gouache. 1908. ". . . the arrangement of a vertical force against a contrasting and balancing horizontal volume." *Photo by Apollo*

enough to strive for perfection. As Coleridge says, strange is this self-power of the imagination.

The lesson of painting has been vital and determinative in the work of Eliel Saarinen. That he was disciplined as a painter may have no technical importance whatever in his work; but, because he subjected himself to the lessons that he found in studying nature and art, Eliel Saarinen knew the degree of perfection he must require of himself. He was an artist because he was so disciplined.

The differences among the expressions of various artists show a considerable range in their concepts of perfection. Without regard for the source of these differences, one can watch the tendencies in various designers to dwell upon a special theme, a line or shape formation, which recurs in their work. Artist-designers translate these thematic tendencies into personal idioms. Though frequently their pencils may produce an aoristic flow of line and shape that carries no significance, at another moment they may create that oft repeated form that identifies itself with a quality somehow inherent in the being of the draftsman.

Where one designer will find this repetition to be an amoebic arrangement, with a side of tension and one of relief in many variations, another will see it in a long, rectilinear volume, which appears, again and again, on his tracing paper. The repetition of such a theme is as revealing of the inner nature of the designer as is the typical Miró or the formations of Picasso. It is the expression of temperament.

59 SKETCH FOR TOWER, CHICAGO LAKE FRONT PLAN. 1923. ". . . the predominating spirit is one of lightness, an upreaching and aspiring strength"

A specific and detailed concern that seems to have occupied Eliel Saarinen's mind, as he bent over the drafting table, is the arrangement of a vertical force against a contrasting and balancing horizontal volume.

In its elementary state this concern shows itself in abstract lines and volumes, which search for harmony in the contrast of upreaching and supporting forces. In practical application, in his furniture, metal, and textile plans, the theme recurs; in his architecture the tendency finds expression in the soaring shaft or the brooding, upsurging mass of tower over a substantial foundation.

Whatever the weight of these masses, Eliel Saarinen created a lightness which, in the towers that he produced, arose with aspiration. Two kinds of towers, those standing free against a background of mass and those intimately associated with the horizontal plane, have been designed by him. In both, the horizontal force of the building and the vertical surge of the tower have a happy proportion, the result of the ability

58 FINNISH PARLIAMENT HOUSE. THE PROJECTED PLAN. 1908. *Photo by Apollo*

50

of the designer combined with the quality of his temperament.

Saarinen's virtuosity with pencil and T-square, developed over a period of years, became a by-word in the designing profession, like that of Frank Lloyd Wright. A thousand times these instruments found their typical expression in his hands by marking out the vertical force against the underlying structure of the supporting mass.

The development of this form—expression in combination with the early discipline in painting—can be followed from the early watercolor sketch of a northern landscape to the final structure of a tower of a church designed for a mid-western American city.

Through his search into the forms of nature Eliel Saarinen found a basic form in architecture. Disregarding the style forms of the prevailing trends in design, he found it necessary to return to fundamental principles which he discovered in nature. As he surveyed the landscape of Finland, the broad pattern of hillside, sea, and valley, he sensed the harmony and the variety in nature. He grasped the meaning of the underlying design structure, which he realized nature could teach him; he laid the foundation upon which he was to build his architectural patterns. In the silhouette of a landscape he comprehended simplicity. This quality he translated into paintings, which contained both natural and man-made forms. He blended the shapes of hills with those of houses. Harmony resulted.

Later, in viewing the structure of a castle or a bridge, Eliel Saarinen came to a personal understanding of the monumental. He saw form as form, no matter what the *literary* content. To achieve this conclusion is the fundamental aim of the artist, no matter what his medium of expression.

The transition was complete, then, between a total view of natural forms and the man-made forms. And, as Saarinen grew in stature, the urge to erect the tower over a solid base made him design, again, the vertical shapes which in so many instances seem to rise sympathetically out of the natural forms surrounding them.

To achieve this balance required many attempts. The number of plans Saarinen drew were sketched many times. In the sketch there is an indication of the procedure—a process of elimination in order to arrive at the right solution—which he used in obtaining the successful blend-

ing of the upward thrust with the level base. Sometimes he worked for days on such a project, discarding a great variety of attempts; sometimes he arrived at a satisfactory conclusion with quick intuition.

The accompanying series of sketches shows a progress toward the final solution of the Landtdagshus, which Eliel Saarinen completed in 1908. A glance at the previous sketches—the landscapes—reveals a similarity between this mass and the natural shapes that one finds in a land of many hills.

In three designs of towers which have been

60 TOWER OF TABERNACLE CHURCH (FIRST CHRISTIAN CHURCH), COLUMBUS, INDIANA. Wash drawing. 1940. ". . . the vertical mass, apart from the main building, is a simple and delicately proportioned form . . ."

selected as illustrative, covering a period of thirty years of Eliel Saarinen's work, the second tower is part of the architectural plan he created for the Chicago lakefront scheme. This tower reveals a spirit completely different from the Finnish parliament building structure; it expresses Saarinen's idea that the design of any building should reflect, to an extent, its environment. In the Chicago project the designer follows a theme much in keeping with the general aspect of the Tribune Tower design. Again, the predominating spirit is one of lightness, an upreaching and aspiring strength.

In the last example, the church tower constructed in Columbus, Indiana, in 1940, the vertical mass, apart from the main building, is a simple and delicately proportioned form, sensitively

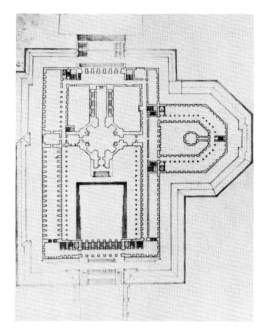

62 KALEVALATALO. FLOOR PLAN. 1921. "His floor plan, unified and closely knit, was the logical base for the tower that he conceived"

supplied with grilles in sparingly applied decoration. With its harmonious base, elongated through its reflection in the adjoining pool, the Tabernacle Church tower is one of the best illustrations of the designer's successful realization of fundamental form.

Eliel Saarinen's art is not yet fully measured in the critic's scales. Time will tell what he accomplished. But his contribution may be grasped more surely if his production is seen in the light of the experiences he recounted here. Thus, the study of the work itself can bring one closer to the spirit of the art and its creator; for, as Eliel Saarinen said, "Form must give forth the spirit; form is the manner in which the spirit is expressed."

10

At the end of the Finnish Civil War in 1918, there arose in the nation a strong unifying force which promised a future for the small country. The cultural forces, powerfully sustained by that spirit which Eliel Saarinen and his friends in Helsingfors had helped to nurture at the turn of the century, gained ascendancy in the life of the new nation.

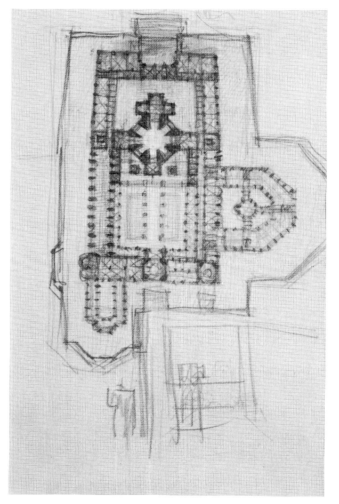

61 KALEVALATALO. PRELIMINARY SKETCH OF FLOOR PLAN. 1921. "... through innumerable stages of development ..."

Inspired by political unity, the Finns wanted a monument dedicated to their cultural achievements. "Every nation, having risen to self-consciousness," said the president of the Kalevala Society in 1921, "loves the past from which it

64 KALEVALATALO. SKETCH. 1921. ". . . a building which would withstand the rigors of these climatic conditions"

63 KALEVALATALO. SKETCHES. 1921

sprang. For a nation which has now reached political independence this future is especially important to establish its security. No culture is independent. For ages the Finns have given and taken from both the east and west. This monument should be the shelter of the rich inheritance of all our nation's cultural wealth." This aspiration of the president of the Kalevala group was a reflection of the hope of all Finland.

In 1893 Saarinen, as a young student, had gone into the countryside of his own area and had discovered many ancient, unrecorded songs and poems of Finnish origin. He became vitally interested in the folk art forms, and in the Kalevala

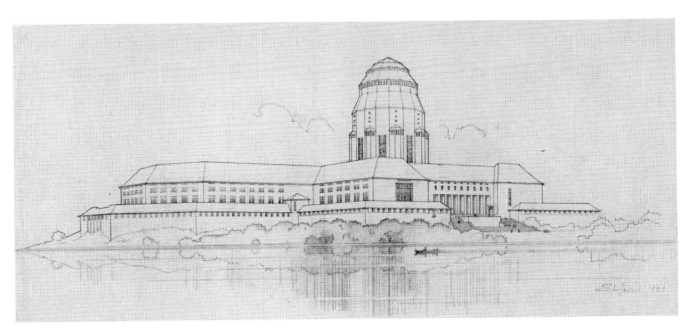

65 KALEVALATALO. SOUTH ELEVATION. 1921. " 'This monument should be the shelter . . . of all our nation's cultural wealth' "

66   KALEVALATALO. AERIAL VIEW. 1921. ". . . a part of a northern landscape . . . intimately at home in its surroundings"

Society he found an outlet for this early concern. It came about that Eliel Saarinen, a member of the Kalevala Society, the organization that fostered the spirit of the nation's unity, was asked to design a great museum to house the folklore of Finland.

A year after the end of the war Saarinen began his design. It was to be a building of tremendous strength, physically and spiritually; the society asked for a structure that would stand as a symbol of the nation's strength in time to come. Saarinen proceeded to work upon a scheme that would fulfil this demand. In his first sketches he visualized a tower outside the main body of the building; in later versions he placed the tower inside the main mass.

Knowing the northern climate, with its heavy snowfall, its deep frosts, and its great variations within the seasons, Eliel Saarinen set out to design a building that would withstand the rigors of these climatic conditions. His floor plan, unified and closely knit, was the logical base for the tower he conceived. After working through the innumerable stages of development, he created

a design that was conditioned to the climate of Finland.

A study of the dimensions of this tower, with its general character of sloping sides, will reveal that Eliel Saarinen's fundamental concern was with the condition of his country's heavy winter. "I tried to meet the severe demands of the northern climate," he said, "as honestly as possible, with that concern as my main and guiding principle."

The structure he suggested, in the final elevation drawings, does seem so thoroughly a part of a northern landscape that it gives the impression of a mountainous solid, intimately at home in its surroundings.

Eliel Saarinen arrived at his selected design through a gradual process of elimination, making innumerable drawings in which he tried various ideas. In the Kalevala project he followed this method, completing drawing upon drawing, first from one elevation and then from another, until he had satisfied himself.

Though this monument was a long-cherished dream in the minds of some Finns, the building

54

will probably never be erected. "Of course, to-day I would alter this design again," the architect said in 1946. "But the day of the Kalevala museum seems to have passed or, perhaps, it is dim in the future."

Following the dissolving of the partnership with Gesellius in 1907, Eliel Saarinen had worked independently toward the forms he felt to be related to the basic and eternal laws of design. After he had gained ascendancy over the forces of the "style" advocates, he was admired by a group of young architects. It was not long, however, before he was again a pioneering force, suspicious alike of romanticism and of a stern classicism which grew up among many young architects during the second decade of the new century. He forged ahead, using materials as he thought best and designing for function as he understood it.

Not being as inventive an engineer as Eero, he did not stress the functional forms by bringing them to the surface. He worked for a harmony between function and material, blending them with his talent for design. He took pleasure in

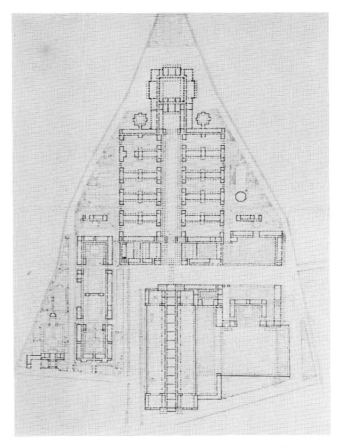

68   CAIRO, EGYPT. HOSPITAL. LAYOUT. 1921

texture and in a personal and discreet ornament. The result was that Saarinen's design at this point of his life was so individual that some, like the American eclectic Swartwout, thought it "naive to the point of Bolshevism."

The Finnish designer was not dismayed, however, by detractors and continued to strive for his ideal of art. He was hard hit financially by the First World War and by the tremendous disturbance within Finland at that time.

There was very little opportunity to build. As Sirén remembered these trying years, "Eliel Saarinen was not able to—nor did he always care to—attend to work on the site with the contractors, as he ought to have done. Partly as a result of this he had no architectural commissions for a few years; he devoted himself to free, artistic production." He painted as a recreation and took part in as many competitions as he could manage. During one of these difficult years he also took on a commission to design paper currency for the new government and nearly ruined his eyesight with the close work it entailed. But the

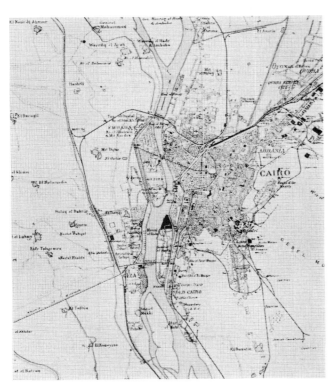

67   CAIRO, EGYPT. GENERAL PLAN OF CAIRO. 1921. ". . . the site was unique—an island on the outskirts of Cairo—invited a different design . . ."

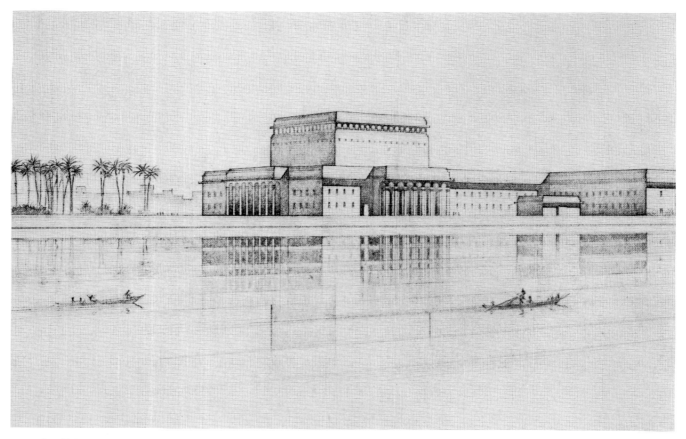

69   CAIRO, EGYPT. HOSPITAL. WEST ELEVATION. DETAIL. 1921. "The pillars . . . bring relief to a solid wall arrangement, which is pierced only infrequently by small windows"

urge to work, constant throughout his life, kept Eliel Saarinen as busy in lean as in prosperous years; he had the "finger-itch" for drawing, as he said.

At the same time that he was designing the Finnish national monument, Saarinen was also working on a design for an international competition for a hospital in Cairo. The hospital plan was a challenge, all its conditions and limitations differing basically from the ones that he faced in his work on the northern monument. It presented an opportunity for the designer to attempt an unsual solution. First, the site was unique—an island on the outskirts of Cairo—which invited a different design from ones he had created for situations in the northern countries. He thought of the site, the climatic conditions, the traditions of the country, the nature of the land, and arrived at an interesting series of plans and elevations.

The ground scheme for the huge buildings—actually a cluster of buildings—shows the designer's usual clarity of expression through the formal, rather austere, disposition of spaces. In the elevation he reveals his concern for the situation of the hospital; the roof of the structure has a helmetlike appearance, an adequate shield against the driving sun.

The pillars, akin in spirit to the Egyptian column although not like it in any specific way, bring relief to a solid wall arrangement pierced only infrequently by small windows. It is likely that, had this structure been built, it would have served its purpose well, and it might have contributed to experimentation in tropical architecture.

In the abstract, Eliel Saarinen analyzed his problem by considering the material which would be readily obtainable, the function of the building, the site, the climate, and the financial conditions stipulated in the competition announcements. He attempted to find an answer and give reasonable consideration to these limitations.

A third design, which may be considered a study of relationship between a building and its

70 CHICAGO. TRIBUNE TOWER. SKETCH. 1922   **71** CHICAGO. TRIBUNE TOWER. SKETCH. 1922

environment, came from the architect's drawing table in 1922. Upon the return of Eliel and Loja Saarinen from a trip to France, the international competition for the Chicago Tribune Tower was announced in grandiloquent terms.

The story of the *Tribune* competition has been told many times, and the second prize that was awarded to the Finnish designer has found mention in the textbooks of the history of Western art. The time came when thoughtful architects turned from this design as a distracting in-influence; skyscraper construction did not seem as desirable as it seemed to be after the First World War.

Whether the skyscraper ever was healthy for any city is a moot question. Before the First World War, the concentration of population within a small area appeared from economic viewpoints to be essential, and the early construction of fairly high office buildings in Chicago and New York had some usefulness. Even today, however, seeing the towers go up in lower Manhattan, one wonders what could stop their growth. However, Eliel Saarinen contributed a

72 CHICAGO. TRIBUNE TOWER. 1922

chapter to the history of the skyscraper. His solution was attractive: the soaring tower with discreet setbacks became a model for a number of buildings now located in various cities.

For the designer this problem was one that gave him another opportunity to attempt to fit his scheme into its environment. He worked under limitations plainly set forth in the instructions which were sent out from Chicago to the competitors. He did not understand completely

and from personal experience the situation of a skyscraper in a distant city in a country he had never visited. For Eliel Saarinen, the plan became ultimately a technical problem in design. He felt that it should not have been built.

He worked fast, often into the night, making the intricate and detailed rendering, piling wash upon wash and erasing and blending the lines of his pen, until he had completed one of the most remarkable drawings in the history of architectural rendering.

The quality of this concept has been thoroughly analyzed by the master designer Louis Sullivan. He quotes the stipulations under which the competition was, supposedly, conducted: "The primary objective of the Chicago Tribune in instituting this competition is to secure the design for a structure distinctive and imposing—'the most beautiful office building in the world.'

"The intensive use of the word *primary*," Sullivan continues, "gives to the full clause the imposing promise of a token, of a covenant with the Earth. With that one word, *primary*, the Tribune set its bow in the cloud.

"Viewed in this light, the second and the first prizes stand before us side by side. One glance of the trained eye, and instant judgment comes; that judgment which flashes from inner experience, in recognition of a masterpiece. . . . The Finnish master-edifice is not a lonely cry in the wilderness, it is a voice, resonant and rich, ringing amidst the wealth and joy of life."

In summary, Sullivan concludes: ". . . there remain, for some, two surprises: first, that a Finlander who, in his prior experience, had had no occasion to design a soaring office building should, as one to the manner born, have grasped the intricate problem of the lofty steel-framed structure . . . second, that a 'foreigner' should possess the insight required to penetrate to the depths of the sound, strong, kindly and aspiring idealism which lies at the core of the American people."[16]

In the light of the history of contemporary architecture the contrasting opinion of Egerton Swartwout is important because it reveals a strong opposition against which a pioneering designer had to work even after he had been at his board for over twenty-five years: "I cannot con-

16. Louis Sullivan, "The Chicago Tribune Competition," *Architectural Record* 53 (February, 1923): 152–53.

sider seriously Mr. Sullivan's statement that the Tribune Building by Saarinen is 'a splendid interpretation of the spirit of the American people,' a statement which to me means nothing. . . ."[17]

For Eliel and Loja Saarinen and for their children the Tribune Tower competition had a more personal importance. It was this event which brought them to the United States. Chicago had no particular significance for them beyond the fact that it was the site of the Columbian Exposition and the home of Louis Sullivan. After he was awarded his prize in the Tribune competition, Eliel Saarinen decided to visit the midwestern American city. A veteran traveler by this time, he looked forward to the trip. Beyond the prospect of seeing a new country, studying new conditions of building, and examining a mode of life with which he was unfamiliar, he had no plans when he embarked for New York.

Economic conditions in Finland were such that the building trade was sluggish. There was little in the future that promised profitable and interesting commissions, and, as Eliel Saarinen was at that time regarded as a designer of the monumental structure requiring considerable outlay of money, there seemed to be few possibilities for him to work.

There may have been, too, a desire to do his work in a country that was not located on the periphery of the main activity in architectural design. The opportunities for contemporary building had improved in Germany. France had a few leaders in the field. The Lowlands were full of promise. But, in America, the turn of

events was soon to demand activity in building construction.

Whatever the combination of motives, Eliel Saarinen left Finland in February 1923 with the intention of visiting colleagues in the United States. In April, Loja, Pipsan, who was then eighteen, and Eero, a lad of thirteen, joined Saarinen in New York. When Eero, already a draftsman trained in his father's studio, saw New York, he spent a sleepless night and reported to his father next morning: "The traffic is all mixed up and wrong. It ought to be changed."

The Saarinen family then went out to the midwest and took up their residence in Evanston, Illinois. Eliel Saarinen was not to spend more than a brief visit now and then to Hvitträsk, for twenty-one years his true home in Finland. "Strong bands always tied the master to this work of his youth," said J. S. Sirén. "One may well grasp his meaning when he, before his voyage to the New World, said to me, 'I am not yet sure that I shall go over there, to entirely new surroundings; or if I shall remain here and dream, below the birch trees of Hvitträsk.' "

Reflecting on this uprooting, Eliel Saarinen recalled with deep emotion, "Hvitträsk was all a home could mean to us; there Pipsan and Eero grew up and there Loja and I were united in that spirit which, I like to think, is the fruit of love."

Though the promises of a new land were fulfilled, it was difficult for Eliel Saarinen and his family to leave Hvitträsk. He did finally return, to remain there forever; Eliel Saarinen's ashes were buried in his home soil at Hvitträsk, Kirkkonummi, Finland, in 1950.

17. Egerton Swartwout, "Review of Recent Architectural Magazines," *American Architect and Architectural Review* 123 (June 20, 1923): 575.

PART TWO

1

ELIEL SAARINEN studied his new home—Chicago. Often he went downtown and saw slums which appalled him behind the lakefront facade of the city.

" 'How do you like Chicago' the conventional question was asked me and so, naturally, I replied, 'I like it, certainly.' But when I took the elevated to the South Side and saw along the tracks the numberless rear 'facades,' all begrimed with smoke and soot, I am afraid I did not like that part of Chicago at all."

Saarinen was shocked when he studied housing conditions in a city which was so young and new by European standards. And he was amazed at the congestion that he found in the streets. When he stayed at the Blackstone Hotel, he frequently crossed Michigan Avenue and, as time passed, found a picture growing in his mind. This picture became rich with detail, and within a few months the Finnish designer was at work on a lakefront plan for downtown Chicago. In a way, this project was a purely academic effort in that Saarinen had consulted no one about the plan. As he said: "I have not aimed to present that plan which shall be executed, but one that can be."

Then, in a small apartment in Evanston, the designer completed his monumental scheme. Thanks to the editor, Page A. Robinson, it was published in *The American Architect* on December 5, 1923, and was acclaimed by a predictive editorial, "street traffic and the storage of automobiles have become the essential factors in city planning. A correct combination of all of these elements must now be included in such undertakings. They are problems that confront every city, town or village which expects to have future growth."

"The city planning project illustrated in this issue is one which incorporates all of these elements. In this project Eliel Saarinen has combined them in such a manner that no interference occurs. The park, with all of the landscape preserved, also serves as a great through-traffic thoroughfare and a parking place for automobiles. The outstanding feature of this project is that traffic and storage are so cleverly disposed of that they do not in any way detract from a beautiful development and use of the park site. This marks it as the greatest advance yet made in city planning . . . one that will become of universal interest."

The main feature of this plan and the paramount concern of the designer was its proposal of a solution for the problem of traffic congestion. This acute condition was relieved in Saarinen's scheme by an automobile terminal, which would have paid for itself and would have given Chicago an underground parking area large enough to have served that city since the 1920s, instead of since the middle 1950s, when the earliest underground parking space became usable.

The architectural aspects of the lakefront plan were not reduced to detail; only the grand masses of proposed structures were suggested, as its designer made clear, "The project is such that future working plans can be made for its successive realization."

Through the years Eliel Saarinen never forgot the conditions in Chicago that so aroused him and Eero when they first saw them. In the 1940s, when he was engrossed in writing his penetrating book *The City*, he devoted a chapter to the midwestern metropolis. Recalling his early lakefront design, he was moved to write that though Lake Shore Drive is "a great achievement of unusual proportions, one cannot refrain from wondering why the face is washed, while the heart remains so dark and cruel." He cared about Chi-

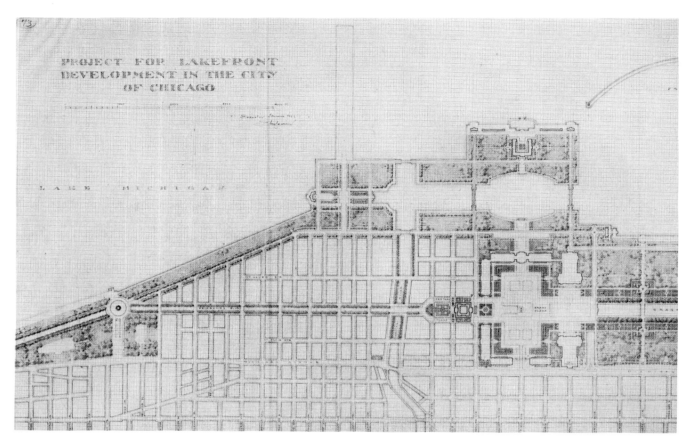

73 CHICAGO LAKE FRONT. GENERAL LAYOUT. 1923. "The main feature of this plan and the paramount con-

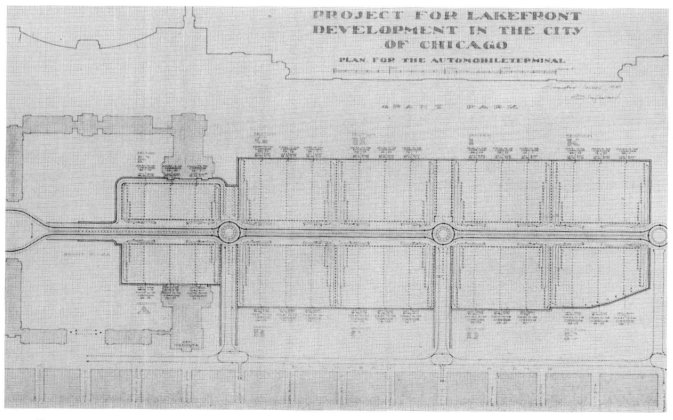

74 CHICAGO LAKE FRONT. THE AUTOMOBILE TERMINAL. 1923. ". . . would have paid for itself . . ."

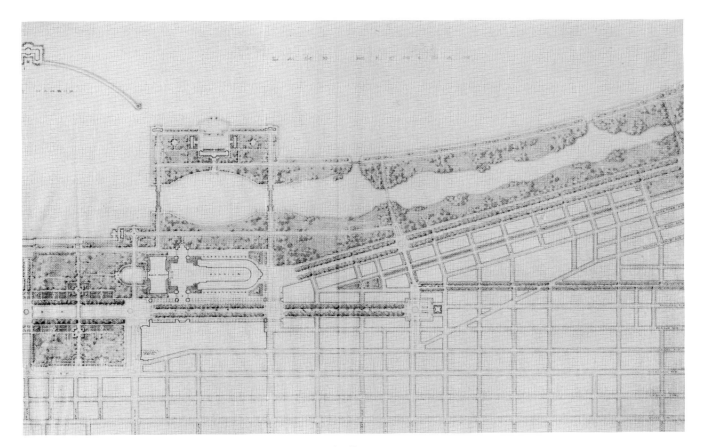

cern of the designer was its solution of the traffic congestion"

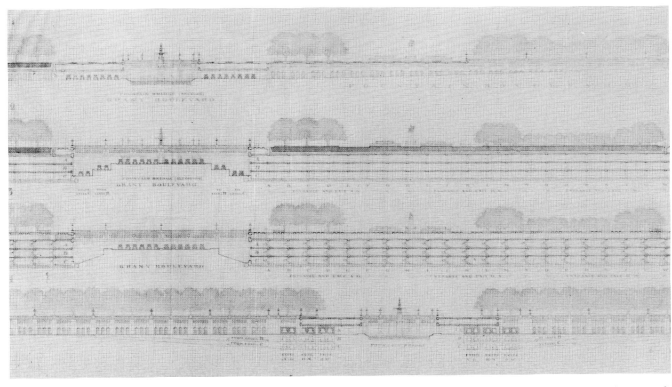

75 CHICAGO LAKE FRONT. SECTIONS OF THE AUTOMOBILE TERMINAL. 1923. ". . . an underground parking area large enough to serve . . . today with efficiency and profit"

76   CHICAGO LAKE FRONT. AERIAL VIEW. CENTRAL PLAZA. 1923. ". . . a monumental scheme . . ."

cago and often spoke about the city.

After he had completed this ambitious and complex job, Eliel Saarinen was asked by Emil Lorch, of the University of Michigan, to join the staff of the architectural school as guest professor. In the autumn of 1923 the Saarinens moved to Ann Arbor, where the designer began his initial work as an educator.

Although he did not realize it then, it was a work to which he was destined to devote a great part of the rest of his life. During his two years at the university and later at Cranbrook, he was involved with teaching for a

quarter of a century. Throughout that period of time, dozens of young architects from many nations came to him as apprentices in design and city planning.

At the University of Michigan the classes "were for advanced students and limited to a small number so that each one would be given individual attention that he might absorb the ideals, philosophy, and methods of approach of this man who for years has been considered one of Europe's great architects. . . . At present he is working on a solution of the Detroit traffic problem which promises to be a farseeing and

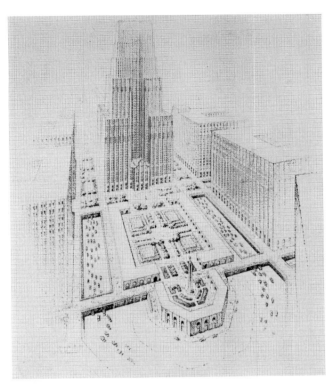

77 CHICAGO LAKE FRONT. AERIAL VIEW. HO-
TEL PLAZA WITH UNDERGROUND RAIL-
ROAD STATION. 1923. ". . . architectural phases
. . . were not reduced to detail; only the large masses
. . . were suggested"

satisfactory project," wrote J. Robert F. Swanson, a student in the school.[1]

Appreciatively aware of the abilities of the
Finnish designer who had been his professor,
young Swanson later introduced him to George
G. Booth, the publisher of the *Detroit News*,
who was interested in a plan for an educational
institution to be built on his estate near Detroit.

Saarinen had, of course, become acquainted
with both Robert Swanson and his classmate
Henry S. Booth while they were studying with
him at the university. After graduation they had
established an office in Bloomfield Hills and near
the end of Saarinen's second year at Ann Arbor
were considering the elder Booth's offer of a job
to design his projected school.

It was natural for Swanson and young Booth
to try to interest their former teacher in their
plans. With some difficulty they persuaded
Saarinen to remain in this country and work
with them on the plans for Cranbrook School.
Both Eliel and Loja were homesick and were
planning to return to Finland at the end of their
second year in Ann Arbor. Until the two young

1. J. Robert F. Swanson, "Eliel Saarinen," *Michigan Technic*
37 (May 1924): 5.

78 CHICAGO LAKE FRONT. SKETCH. SUNKEN TRAFFIC ARTERY THROUGH GRANT PARK. 1923

79 BLOOMFIELD HILLS, MICHIGAN. CRANBROOK SCHOOL FOR BOYS. AERIAL VIEW. 1925. ". . . a combination of various influences . . . worked upon the architect, and from the sum of these he began his drawings"

architects appeared, there had been no substantial offers to enlist Saarinen's talents outside the classroom. So, he agreed to work with them on designing the first building at Cranbrook School for Boys.

While this work was in progress, Robert Swanson and Pipsan were married. From 1924 on, the young architect was associated on numerous jobs with his father-in-law. Naturally,

the most important of these was the design and development of the early Cranbrook buildings. He contributed to the first Detroit Riverfront Development, the Alexander Hamilton Memorial in Chicago, and some of the designs Eliel executed for International Silver.

The Detroit riverfront plan was the first of three designs that Eliel Saarinen drew up for this midwestern industrial center. Naturally, it was related to the proposal he had created in Chicago. He said, "Having so brief an experience with the problems of the industrial centers of this country, I thought in terms of my previous solutions. While I feel, in retrospect, that I paid attention to some basic needs of the city, such as Detroit, I used the same layouts and building plans which I brought with me. However, I learned. My concern for the Detroit riverfront was to continue; Eero inherited it and worked on it after 1947."

The plan that he conceived in 1924 consisted of a central structure with a dome, which Saarinen arranged in the foreground as a memorial hall. A long wing on the right of this building was to be the exposition hall and a convention

auditorium. The architectural climax of the group of buildings was to be a tower building, an imposing shaft facing the water. But the stern and grandiose design of the buildings was not the important aspect of this plan; the designer's main concern was the traffic problem, solved by means of an esplanande, triple-decked, with a subway station and automobile parking area under the decks.

In commenting on his change in concept and techniques in dealing with the redesign of the city, Eliel Saarinen revealed his ability to grow, to match his ideas to meet the need of the time. His colleagues and students might place this quality of adaptability uppermost among his characteristics for, in each lesson he taught or

80 CRANBROOK SCHOOL FOR BOYS. CORNER OF QUADRANGLE. 1925. ". . . rational grouping . . ."

81 CRANBROOK SCHOOL FOR BOYS. DETAIL OF PERGOLA, 1925. ". . . uses of personal . . . patterns upon pillars, archways, doors . . ." *Photo by Nyholm*

82 CRANBROOK SCHOOL FOR BOYS. COURT VIEW. 1925. ". . . the sensitive use of pattern in the brick . . ." *Photo by Nyholm*

83 CRANBROOK SCHOOL FOR BOYS. WITH SCULPTURE BY MILLES. 1925. *Photo by Nyholm*

84 CRANBROOK SCHOOL FOR BOYS. DINING HALL. 1925. *Photo by Harvey Croze*

85 CRANBROOK SCHOOL FOR BOYS. EAST GATEWAY. 1925. *Photo by Askew*

in the suggestions he offered, he reserved the right to change his mind. He would not impose a dogma on the mind of his associates; he was too witty to be pedantic.

With an interest in the arts and crafts, in education and religion, George G. Booth, with his strength and wealth, had already begun a training center for artists that was unique in America. Since the turn of the century, often in association with his brother Ralph, he had given generously to support arts and crafts in the Detroit area. Having given scholarships to young American architects and artists to attend the academies of Europe, Booth studied the results of his philanthropy and became convinced that such educational aid was faulty. The time that the student from the United States should have de-

voted to a study of his culture with the aim of ultimately contributing intelligently to it was spent in a superficial study of a form foreign to him, which could result only in imitative reconstructions. Only a few at that time sensed this dilemma of the American art student.

Basing his thoughts upon the experience he had gathered in his early work as a metal designer, his study of a number of Detroit's art institutions, and his own experiments in supporting various movements of arts and crafts at his Cranbrook home, Booth decided to launch upon a more ambitious enterprise than he had until that time contemplated.

At its very beginning, the movement that resulted in the building of Cranbrook Academy of Art was merely a gathering of artisans and

86 KINGSWOOD SCHOOL, CRANBROOK. AERIAL VIEW. 1929. ". . . designed altogether by the architect and by his family." *Photo by Arnold*

87 KINGSWOOD SCHOOL, CRANBROOK. VIEW FROM CRANBROOK LAKE. 1929. ". . . a lake . . . a wooded hillside offered an intimate inclosure." *Photo by Hance*

88 KINGSWOOD SCHOOL, CRANBROOK. FRONT ELEVATION. Gouache. 1929. "The mass of the buildings . . . in conformity with the general contour of the shore land . . ."

craftsmen. They were assembled to work on a country home for the Booths, who in 1904 had pioneered in developing the suburban area, Bloomfield Hills, Michigan. A continuously increasing plan demanded the construction of a meetinghouse where the children of the neighborhood could attend school and Sunday services. From the modest beginning of this meetinghouse the interest of George G. Booth and his wife Ellen Scripps Booth turned to other educational and religious projects until, in 1927, the Cranbrook Foundation was created. The community of institutions had grown to include a church, a well-equipped school for all children, a school for boys, and shops for arts and crafts, which were destined to develop steadily into an

organized art center, the Academy of Art.

Not with any well-defined idea about the ultimate form of the institution but with a general plan of creating a place in which artists might work in privacy and in adequate studios located in a pleasant environment. the publisher laid the early foundation for the Cranbrook Academy of Art. The Finnish designer was consulted, and at the conclusion of the conference, the two decided to work together in developing these plans. No preconceptions guided them; during the years from 1926 to 1943, a gradual plan evolved which produced four Cranbrook institutions.

Eliel Saarinen began his first executed architectural work in the United States—the Cran-

89 KINGSWOOD SCHOOL, CRANBROOK. DORMITORY. 1929. ". . . ascending and descending in a series of levels . . ." *Photo by Hance*

90 KINGSWOOD SCHOOL, CRANBROOK. LIBRARY TERRACE. 1929. ". . . harmony between material and function . . ." *Photo by Hance*

91 KINGSWOOD SCHOOL, CRANBROOK. MAIN ENTRANCE. 1929. ". . . observation of nature translated into terms of architectural design." *Photo by Hance*

brook School for Boys—in 1925 in association with Robert Swanson. Swanson was so enthusiastic about this opportunity that he pledged his own fee for the boys' school contract to pay for Eliel Saarinen's salary the first year.

The plot plan of the school shows a rational grouping of buildings around well-proportioned courts. The elaborate structures are in beautiful scale relation to one another.

A major consideration in developing this design was Booth's stipulation that the original group of farm buildings on the site, which had no particular character, was to be remodeled and that additional buildings should harmonize with this group. The limitations thus placed upon the architect had a determining effect on the design in all its major features.

Reaching out for a larger solution to the problem, pressed by the requirements of a rapid expansion and by the client's increasing interest, Eliel Saarinen went on to extend his original scheme. For this larger design Loja Saarinen built a model of amazing fidelity and detail. When it was completed, the plan was presented to George G. Booth, and it was decided that the school would be developed to the extent to which the architect had visualized it. It was, in general character, to be sympathetic with the lines of the farm buildings and adjusted to the client's profound interest in the arts and crafts movement.

The plot of the Cranbrook School for Boys followed the suggestion of the arrangement of the buildings and yards of the farm, and so the character of the school was further determined. All in all, it was a combination of various influences working upon the architect, and from the sum of these he began his drawings.

The proportions and arrangement of the buildings, the sensitive use of pattern in the brick, the decorative detail, reveal the designer's adaptability. Most interesting are his uses of personal and warm patterns upon pillars, archways, doors, and interiors. The experience of years of designing is expressed in these details. But the design as a whole is not the work of Eliel Saarinen; he was reserved about it.

This first completed work of Eliel Saarinen in his new environment is one which is the logical outcome of the orientation process through which the designer passed during his initial years in the United States. With a receptive mind he willingly attempted to equip himself for the years ahead; he had either to do this or to find frustration in the unhappy circumstances of his life because of fixed and unbending ideas about

92 KINGSWOOD SCHOOL, CRANBROOK. DETAILS OF MAIN ENTRANCE. 1929. "The achievement of a distinctive form . . ." *Photo by Hance*

93 KINGSWOOD SCHOOL, CRANBROOK. MAIN AUDITORIUM. 1929. *Photo by Habrecht*

94 KINGSWOOD SCHOOL, CRANBROOK. DINING HALL. 1929. " '. . . harmony . . . of collaborative artists . . .' "

design. Eliel Saarinen always chose the way of learning and of new development. He began to create new forms for a new condition.

2

Immediately after the school for boys had been completed, the plan for the art academy was developed. In the first stages of the growth of this institution, the arts and crafts buildings followed the design of the first school.

After spending the summer of 1928 in Finland, where Eliel and Loja Saarinen visited each year from the time of their arrival in Michigan until the Second World War, the architect drew up the plan for the Saarinen home at Cranbrook. Following his practice in Hvitträsk twenty years before, Saarinen designed the complete interior of the house and the furniture, which was built

95 KINGSWOOD SCHOOL, CRANBROOK. STAIR-WELL. 1929. *Photo by Hance*

96 KINGSWOOD SCHOOL, CRANBROOK. CLASSROOM CORRIDOR. 1929. " '. . . the collaboration of several individuals . . . achieved . . . a unification of motif, color, and texture . . ." *Photo by Hance*

in the woodworking shops of the new arts and crafts center. Loja, who was then busy developing one of the most productive modern weaving departments in the United States, designed and wove the draperies, rugs, and the upholstery for the furniture.

This development at Cranbrook was of greater importance than the architect and his wife realized. The client, seeing the quality of these creations, suggested an idea for a school for girls which should be designed altogether by the architect and his family. In Kingswood School, planned in 1929, the wealth of the mature concepts of both Eliel and Loja Saarinen was given full expression. Eero and Pipsan participated in this extensive program.

"The success or failure of practically every architectural effort is largely dependent upon the collaboration of a group of individuals," said the *Architectural Forum* in evaluating this completed project. "In the contemplation of an architectural project significantly successful in both the conception of the design and its execution may be recognized the guiding hand of a master designer working in the closest possible harmony with the representatives of whatever collaborative artists may be involved.

"It is unnecessary to characterize the designer of the Kingswood School, for the abilities of Eliel Saarinen need no introduction to any architect either in America or abroad; and the Kingswood School as the latest example of his work needs little comment as an exemplification of his designing genius. It is significant, however, as one of the most pointed lessons in cooperative designing which we have been fortunate enough to present for some time."[2]

Not only is this judgment interesting as an indication of the enthusiasm with which this work was received; more than that, it is the announcement of the success of Eliel Saarinen and of Loja in the search for the idiom that was to develop richly during the following years. In Kingswood the new creativity of the Saarinens was revealed. From this point on, the work of the designer and his wife was remarkable for its youthful, adventuresome, and yet completely mature nature. Kingswood School is a milestone in the career of both Eliel and Loja Saarinen.

2. "The Kingswood School for Girls, Cranbrook, Michigan," *Architectural Forum* 56 (January 1932): 37.

They had studied America for five years; their new form was evolving.

Working in collaboration with George G. Booth and his wife, the Saarinens determined the particular needs of this school for girls, which was to be located on a site of unusual qualities: a lake fronted the area upon which the school was to be erected while in the background a wooded hillside offered an intimate enclosure.

Taking advantage of this setting, the designer planned the foundations with an eye to the functional aspects of the school. An easy circulatory system and an intelligent disposition of the dormitory and work areas were fitted to the form of the natural surroundings. The mass of the buildings is horizontal, in conformity with the general contour of the shore land, ascending and descending in a series of levels which takes cognizance of the gradual slope of the land.

The deeper meaning of the victory of the designer in his search for form is stated in a sentence of the reviewer's text, which, quite unconsciously, expressed the full measure of Eliel Saarinen's achievement in Kingswood: "There has been no effort to achieve a startlingly different or individualistic scheme of architectural design—a fact which may account largely for the undoubted success of the building."[3] This was one of the most welcome evaluations that the architect received. He often mentioned this as a milestone in the life of the Saarinen family in the new land.

3. *Ibid.*, p. 38.

97 KINGSWOOD SCHOOL, CRANBROOK. LIBRARY. 1929. ". . . co-operative designing . . . toward a common objective . . ." *Photo by Habrecht*

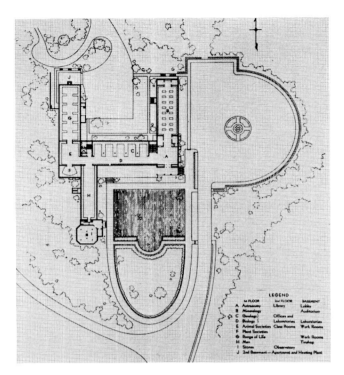

98 CRANBROOK INSTITUTE OF SCIENCE. 1931

In the realization of his mature years Eliel Saarinen achieved that individuality which is in harmony with what he called "fundamental forces." The structure of Kingswood invites a comparison with the form of plants. Like a plant, this building pushes upward from the soil, reaching for air and light. Situated upon a solid, sure base, the structure rises and unfolds, disclosing its charm. Throughout the series of buildings the plastic, decorative details emerge,

not one among them associated with the stereotyped manner of the past and yet each, like the flower, a subtle variation of the others. The harmony between material and function, proportion and decoration is, in this project, a revelation of what may be accomplished when head and heart work together.

Perhaps, in Kingswood, Eliel Saarinen realized the benefit of all his observation of nature, translated into terms of architectural design. Without any guide except the "fundamental principle," he achieved a distinctive form. Only from nature could the designer receive the lessons that were required upon which to base such judgment.

"The plant grows from its seed. The characteristics of its form lie concealed in the potential power of the seed. The soil gives it strength to grow, and the outer influences decide its shape in the environment," he said.

For Loja Saarinen this project of staggering proportions was an opportunity to do the most extensive work of her career as designer and weaver. With the assistance of Maija Wirde, a Swedish artist, she designed the rugs, the curtains, and the furniture covering for the Kingswood interiors. Working for a year, supervising the labor of a dozen weavers, she completed this monumental task for the opening of the school year in 1931.

Pipsan and Eero, educated in design by their parents almost without their realization of being trained, were capable of helping Eliel and Loja Saarinen in many of the details of this structure.

99 CRANBROOK INSTITUTE OF SCIENCE. AERIAL VIEW. 1931. *Photo by Askew*

100 CRANBROOK INSTITUTE OF SCIENCE. FRONT VIEW. 1931. "... a research center ... modest and compact ... effective as a working instrument of display and scholarship." *Photo by Askew*

101 CRANBROOK INSTITUTE OF SCIENCE. MAIN ENTRANCE. 1931. "The occasional ornament is discreetly placed." *Photo by Askew*

102 CRANBROOK INSTITUTE OF SCIENCE. 1931.
". . . a steady development toward simpler forms."
Photo by Askew

The daughter decorated the auditorium and ball-room interiors; the son designed the furniture. It is in Kingswood that the effect of cooperative designing and of individuals working toward a common objective is most clearly illustrated.

"Not so noteworthy is the unusual fact that the architect's family collaborated with him in the interior decoration and furnishing of the Kingswood School as is the fact that designers other than the architect were intimately concerned with important parts of the project. The salient thing in this connection is that the collaboration of several individuals who have worked with each other long enough to recognize the predominating trend in an architectural problem have achieved in their individual fields a unification of motif, color, and texture which would have been impossible otherwise. As a result the entire design of the Kingswood School is eminently consistent."[4]

Eliel Saarinen, walking through the corridors of Kingswood with Frank Lloyd Wright, was amused to hear the visitor exclaim: "You always have the luck to work with good materials, while I seem always to have to work with lesser ones." He was thankful for George G. Booth!

4. *Ibid.*, p. 39.

The success of the Kingswood School project prompted the client in the year following the dedication to ask the designer to create plans for the Cranbrook Institute of Science, an organization engaged in extensive projects of scientific research and display. The plot plan for the science museum was made in 1931; the structure was completed in 1933.

With funds strictly limited, the architect attained an original concept for an exhibition building and research center which, while modest and compact, is effective as a working instrument of display and scholarship. His initial idea was to create a more open and a lighter facade than was eventually erected. As it stands today, though unfortunately altered to accommodate the pressure of growth, the building still is an attractive, functional museum and laboratory, simple and unostentatious, a fitting home for its exhibition galleries and study rooms.

Occasional ornaments are discreetly placed. Most of the decorative designs which are characteristic of the architect are present in the columns that face the building. Calculated to catch a pattern of light and cast shadow, they relieve the severity of the horizontal mass of the main structure.

As was his habit at Cranbrook, Eliel Saarinen supervised the construction of this building. He had a love for the proper arrangement of brick, and he spent many hours in directing the workmen to put up a wall in a way which would satisfy him. "The careless bricklayer is a menace to good texture," he said. "The brick must not be laid too mechanically nor too recklessly. No matter how well your drawings look on the drafting board, it is the construction men who give the finesse to the design, eventually."

The institute building is asymmetrical in plan, with an entrance porch on the south. Adjacent is the reflecting pool, a device typical of many of the designs of Eliel Saarinen, giving movement and life to the total; this pool holds playful Triton figures by Carl Milles.

In the interior of the science building the designer reduced the surfaces to the simple terms he thought appropriate to the purposes of the museum. Here is suggested the impersonal and objective nature of the scientist for whom this structure was erected.

Said Robert T. Hatt, for many years the director of the institute: "We worked to create a building that would set a new standard for natural history museum buildings. The visitors who have come from other science museums are invariably impressed by the refreshing treatment of the design achieved by Eliel Saarinen."

3

The year 1929 was one of far-reaching significance for the Cranbrook community. It was the year Carl Milles visited there and was asked by Eliel Saarinen to become the resident sculptor and director of the department of sculpture at the academy. Milles consented, and within a few months he returned to Michigan where he took the studio in which he achieved the climax of his life's work.

The collaboration between the architect and the Swedish sculptor, which has brought many monumental works to the Cranbrook center, began during these first years of the establishment of the academy, of which Eliel Saarinen was appointed president in 1932. Only Sweden can claim as large a number of sculptures by Carl Milles as can be found today on the campus of the Cranbrook institutions.

The comprehensive plan that Eliel Saarinen visualized in 1931 was the foundation for the Cranbrook Academy of Art. He expressed his ideas concerning the educational structure of the institution after five years of study.

"When fully developed, the Academy of Art is planned to include departments of architecture, design, drawing, painting, sculpture, landscape design, drama, music, and crafts.

103 CRANBROOK ACADEMY OF ART. CRAFTS BUILDING. 1928. "At its very beginning the Cranbrook Academy of Art was a gathering of artisans and craftsmen . . ." *Photo by Harvey Croze*

104 CRANBROOK ACADEMY OF ART. STUDIOS. 1931–32. ". . . the grasp of the fundamental idea that an artist must produce something." *Photo by Harvey Croze*

"The Academy of Art group will include buildings for various purposes, such as museums for painting and for sculpture, for collections of contemporary art from various countries, for collections of building materials. In the Academy group will be an auditorium and lecture rooms, assembly and clubrooms, a dining hall, an art library, theater, music hall; studios for general use for visiting artists, living quarters for artists and craftsmen, studies for weaving and textile designing, cabinet work, metal work, pottery, book printing and binding.

"The Cranbrook Academy of Art is not an art school in the ordinary sense. It is a working place for creative people. The leading idea is to have artists of highest ability live at Cranbrook and execute their work there. Those artists form a more or less permanent staff of the Art Council. Beside these artists, we shall have living quarters and studios for visiting artists who will stay at Cranbrook for a year, six months, or so. These visiting artists from various parts of the country or from foreign countries will bring freshness and new impulses to the institution and will help us to a richer and closer understanding of the contemporary movement in various minds and in various countries.

"No doubt this rich and creative atmosphere will bring to Cranbrook young artists and art students who are eager to develop their talents. They will have their private studios, where they do their own work; and in being continuously in close contact with the master-artists, they can learn from them how to develop their own individualities.

"Creative art cannot be taught by others. Each one has to be his own teacher. But connection with the other artists and discussions with them provide sources for inspiration.

"To develop an Academy of Art in a direction as outlined above is a slow process. The problem has to be carefully studied, and the right men have to be found.

"How much we can do, we do not know. The buildings will not do the work. The artists we can get to live at Cranbrook do the work partly, but most depends on the artistic creative power of the youth of the country. However, we do think the time is ripe for such an institution, and we have hopes for its success."

With his knowledge of what kind of art center was needed at the time, Eliel Saarinen, assisted by his colleagues, began to build upon the foundation that he had laid in his philosophy about the nature of the institution. That his

thoughts were realistic is demonstrated today; the general form of the institution he visualized exists upon the campus of the Cranbrook Academy of Art.

President Wallace Mitchell said, a quarter of a century after Eliel Saarinen retired as president, "We have completed a most satisfying year; the program, evidence shows, works wonderfully well. Eliel Saarinen saw ahead so clearly; the Academy continues his ideas and justifies his faith."

It took a decade to complete the construction of the academy. With the exception of his plans for music and drama, Eliel's concepts for the educational structure and his blueprints for the physical structure were followed faithfully in the development of Cranbrook Academy of Art.

When he had established the weaving studios, which gained international renown under the guidance of Loja Saarinen and Marianne Strengell, the sculpture and ceramic studios, the design department, and the architectural planning division, the task of the architect, when he be-

105 CRANBROOK ACADEMY OF ART. SAARINEN AND MILLES RESIDENCES AND STUDIOS. 1929. ". . . after nearly twenty years a testimony to their way of living, personal and professional." *Photo by Harvey Croze*

came president of the academy of art in 1932, was to expand the work of the academy, to design the buildings required for housing students and faculty, and to provide working quarters for them.

During the years he served as head of the academy, Eliel Saarinen not only planned buildings but, according to his original view, also promoted the expansion of the educational organization, adding to the academy the department of painting under the supervision of Zoltan Sepeshy and Wallace Mitchell, the design shop under Charles Eames and Eero Saarinen, the metalwork department under Harry Bertoia, and the ceramic studio supervised by Maija Grotell.

After he had founded his department of postgraduate architecture and city planning in 1930, Eliel Saarinen was able, as instructor, to give expression to that idealistic part of his personality which made him an inspiring teacher and leader. From all parts of the world he brought students to Cranbrook, serious and ambitious architects who wished to continue and broaden their training.

The architecture and city planning department, to which he devoted every moment he could take from his own work, was a laboratory for research work in design, architecture, and planning, where the talented architect supplemented the formal education he had previously received at a college of architecture. The basic theory of Eliel Saarinen's teaching was that the student must have a specific problem when he arrived at Cranbrook and that, during his stay, he must achieve a solution for his problem.

His views were discussed in an article published by *Architectural Record* in June 1933:

"Eliel Saarinen's philosophy of architectural

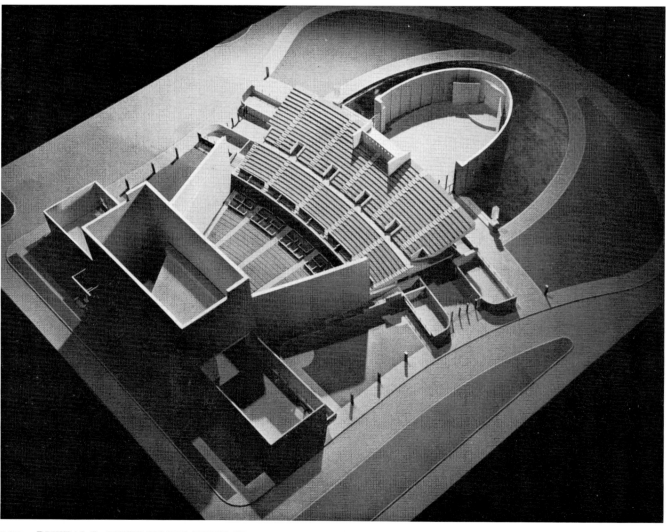

106 BUFFALO, NEW YORK. KLEINHANS MUSIC HALL. MODEL. 1938. *Photo by Askew*

education includes the premise that all work done by the student must be based upon reality, and therefore be a part of life itself, and not upon artificial conditions about which the student can only theorize. Architecture, according to Mr. Saarinen, is not necessarily building, but it includes everything which man has created as a practical organic solution of his relation to his environment. The student at Cranbrook must think, feel, and understand architecture not as a 'fine art,' but as something with which man has constant contact. Each student at Cranbrook chooses his own problem which he develops to a solution. These problems as chosen are those in which the student has a vital interest and thorough knowledge of the surroundings and conditions of life which may have an influence on the solution. These may be a plan of his home city, a development project for a specific location, or even a commission for a client's residence. They are individual problems and are developed as actual jobs. In this the student has the advantage of learning from the problems of

109 BUFFALO, NEW YORK. KLEINHANS MUSIC HALL. AERIAL VIEW. 1938. " 'The shape of the violin,' said Eliel Saarinen, 'has not derived from a preconceived style form.' " *Photo by Damora*

107 BUFFALO, NEW YORK. KLEINHANS MUSIC HALL. WASH DRAWING. ELEVATION WITHOUT STAGE. 1938

108 BUFFALO, NEW YORK. KLEINHANS MUSIC HALL. WASH DRAWING. ELEVATION FROM POOL, WITH STAGE. 1938

his associates and by their mutual criticism. There is no assembling of stylistic forms for the solution of a problem, but a dependence upon common sense."[5]

Eliel Saarinen's philosophy of art education was, by and large, the educational policy of the academy in all its departments. The results in student and faculty production justified the principles; the students who completed their work in the school furnished evidence that this training program had been soundly constructed.

"We are about to begin a new year," Eliel Saarinen once said at a September meeting of students and faculty. "When I arrived here, things were different. There were only pigs and chickens on these acres. Now you are here and—what an improvement!

"We have buildings which give you oppor-

5. "An Announcement of the Third Post-graduate Program at Cranbrook, Architectural Department," *Architectural Record* 63 (June 1933): 431–32.

110 BUFFALO, NEW YORK. KLEINHANS MUSIC HALL. MAIN ENTRANCE. 1938. *Photo by Damora*

111 BUFFALO, NEW YORK. KLEINHANS MUSIC HALL. CHAMBER MUSIC HALL. 1938. *Photo by Damora*

112 BUFFALO, NEW YORK. KLEINHANS MUSIC HALL. MAIN FAÇADE. 1938. *Photo by Askew*

113 BUFFALO, NEW YORK. KLEINHANS MUSIC HALL. MAIN AUDITORIUM. 1938. *Photo by Askew*

tunity to work. But the buildings are nothing, the studios are nothing, unless you use them to full advantage.

"Next May there will be an exhibition of your work. Though many things may happen between now and then which you may think important, these are of little consequence. The only thing that matters is this: Will the exhibition in May be a good one? If so, this year will be counted a successful one; if not, it will have been a failure."

To this day the annual exhibition of student work is evidence of the success of the activities at Cranbrook Academy. And so Eliel Saarinen would want it. "Art cannot be taught; it must be learned. What you learn shows here."

What Eliel Saarinen's graduate students learned and how successful they were may be measured by their later acclaim in the fields of architecture, planning, and design. When their

professional attainments are considered, Saarinen's contribution as an educator appears to have been noteworthy and influential. His most famous pupil was no doubt his son Eero, who worked with him longest. His son-in-law, J. Robert F. Swanson, one of his earliest students in this country, was, of course, closely allied with him in several ways. Other students who went to Cranbrook to study with him, and who achieved greatly, are Carl Feiss, Charles Eames, Harry Weese, Florence Knoll-Bassett, Ralph Rapson, Edmund Bacon, Benjamin Baldwin, Gyo Obata, George Matsumoto, and Donald R. Knorr.

4

Because both Eliel and Loja Saarinen had always been accustomed to a home in which they expressed themselves by designing the interior, the furniture, and the household equipment, they welcomed the opportunity to build their residence at Cranbrook in 1928.

After their arrival in the United States, the Saarinens had worked and lived in makeshift quarters; they had not felt altogether at home since they departed from Hvitträsk. At Cranbrook they set out to create an environment characteristic of their way of living—personal and professional.

Working with the new forms, which came to them as they grew accustomed to their life in the new country, Eliel and Loja Saarinen planned a house which, while it was not of a scale similar to that of the home in Finland, was impressive in proportion and convenient for them both.

The house was divided into two parts: the front of the structure facing the street of the academy contained the living quarters, while the wing at the back joined Eliel Saarinen's studio with the classrooms of his architectural department for graduate students during his regime.

When the structure was completed, in 1929, the Saarinens began to fill the rooms with furnishings of their own design and making. After a few years of patient work, the home assumed that distinctive quality which betokened the taste

114 BUFFALO, NEW YORK. KLEINHANS MUSIC HALL. DETAIL OF CHAMBER MUSIC HALL. 1938. *Photo by Damora*

of the designer and his wife. Almost every article in the house had been produced by the Saarinens, by their children, or by artists of their acquaintance.

Loja Saarinen, supervising the designing and weaving of the textile fabrics, furnished the house with rugs, draperies, and upholstery. Most of the furniture was designed by her husband and built in the woodwork shops at the academy. Metalwork and incidental woodwork, glass, and hardware were all patterned by the architect, as were the terraces and much of the landscaping about the residence. Under his supervision the silver and brass serving pieces used in the dining room were manufactured. During subsequent years some chairs designed by Eero Saarinen and by Alvar Aalto were added.

The patterns characteristic of Loja Saarinen, usually geometric in shape and subdued in color, were unified with the hues and values that were her trademark: warm yellow, tan, and brown, with complementary cool colors in subtle dark and light schemes. The total effect of the interior of the home was a richness in variety, a harmonious unity of form that was the result of a Saarinen collaboration.

In 1929 Eliel Saarinen was asked to take part in an exhibition, "The Architect and Industrial Art," sponsored by the Metropolitan Museum. The project he conceived was a complete dining room; a number of pieces of silver, which were manufactured later by the International Silver Company and Reed and Barton, were created for this exhibition. Included in the tableware was Saarinen's invention, the short-bladed table knife.

In the Metropolitan project the architect indicated again his concept of design—the fundamental molding force so notable among Finnish architects—which could shape matter, whether metal for utility and ornament in the home or building material for architectural construction. Design, in such complete employment, creates totality.

Design is the foundation upon which the structure is built; design is the grammar of art, and so Eliel Saarinen considered it throughout his lifetime.

There was no hiatus in Eliel Saarinen's work when he dealt with various materials which may serve very different functions. "To me there must be a unity of concept here," he said, "oth-erwise the personality of the artist can only be fragmentary."

Eliel Saarinen thought of personality as the wellspring of all creation. Because he was concerned with personality, he was more than an architect; he was an educator. In his relations with designers, certainly throughout his Cranbrook years, he devoted as much thought to the quality of man as to the characteristics of his product. He penetrated to the underlying source.

"It is fundamental," Eliel Saarinen observed, "that whatever forms a man brings forth through honest work, those forms will not be altogether convincing unless they are a true expression of his life—his emotions, his thoughts, and his aspirations. His art, at best, is a significant testimony of his integrity of mind and spirit, the product of his real personality. No work of art in any

115 BUFFALO, NEW YORK. KLEINHANS MUSIC HALL. CHAMBER MUSIC HALL. 1938. ". . . vital problems of function . . ." *Photo by Askew*

116 BUFFALO, NEW YORK. KLEINHANS MUSIC HALL. MEZZANINE. 1938. *Photo by Askew*

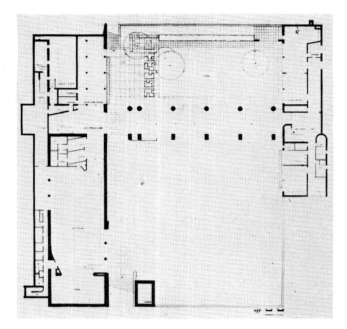

117 COLUMBUS, INDIANA. TABERNACLE CHURCH OF CHRIST (FIRST CHRISTIAN CHURCH). SUNKEN TERRACE PLAN. 1940

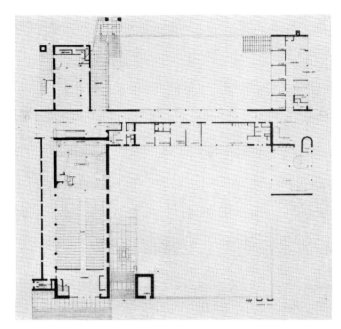

119 COLUMBUS, INDIANA. TABERNACLE CHURCH OF CHRIST (FIRST CHRISTIAN CHURCH). MAIN FLOOR PLAN. 1940

field can be considered a work of art unless it reveals the basic nature of the artist himself."

It was the effect of this lesson upon Eero and Pipsan that brought them, as children, to appreciate the nature of the job they had to do, no matter how complex. Such root principles were their guide rules. They proceeded to their mature work with confidence. The result has been a production of outstanding quality in industrial

design, furniture, interior design, textiles and draperies, painting, sculpture, and architecture. Eero was tireless; a genius was stopped in mid-career when he died at fifty-one on September 1, 1961. Pipsan, associated with her husband's and her son's architectural office, continues to design, specializing in interiors and furniture.

In 1935, in the gallery of the Cranbrook Academy of Art, the Saarinen family exhibited

118 COLUMBUS, INDIANA. TABERNACLE CHURCH OF CHRIST (FIRST CHRISTIAN CHURCH). SUNKEN GARDEN WITH POOL. 1940. *Rendering by Eames*

120 COLUMBUS, INDIANA. TABERNACLE CHURCH OF CHRIST (FIRST CHRISTIAN CHURCH). NAVE. 1940. *Rendering by Eames*

a collection of objects they had created. Family groups working in one profession have existed, of course, in many fields; but such outstanding production by the members of a family, each in his own medium, is nonetheless, rare enough to be given special notice. The elder Saarinens inspired Pipsan and Eero to achieve what they did; it was their daily example that instructed their gifted children.

5

After Eero Saarinen had graduated from the Yale School of Architecture in 1934, he began to work in his father's studio and to teach design at the academy, preparing to assume the directorship of the architectural department. Since Eero had grown up in the atmosphere of the world Eliel Saarinen and his associates had created, it was a natural thing for the son to continue his association with his father in the studio after he returned from his years of formal training in New Haven and after some years of work in the east. Since the time when Eero had helped his father with the drafting of elevations for the Chicago lakefront project, he had been an assistant in the architectural studio where he watched the progress of the designs for the Cranbrook buildings.

121 COLUMBUS, INDIANA. TABERNACLE CHURCH OF CHRIST (FIRST CHRISTIAN CHURCH). FRONT ELEVATION. 1940. ". . . meets the requirements of the congregation today." *Photo by Hedrich-Blessing*

122 COLUMBUS, INDIANA. TABERNACLE CHURCH OF CHRIST (FIRST CHRISTIAN CHURCH). VIEW OF BIBLE SCHOOL. 1940. "The bridge, supported by columns, contains two floors of the church school." *Photo by Hedrich-Blessing*

123 COLUMBUS, INDIANA. TABERNACLE CHURCH OF CHRIST (FIRST CHRISTIAN CHURCH). ENTRANCE TO BIBLE SCHOOL. 1940. ". . . space for the many services the church would offer to the community . . ." *Photo by Hedrich-Blessing*

124 COLUMBUS, INDIANA. TABERNACLE CHURCH OF CHRIST (FIRST CHRISTIAN CHURCH). MAIN AUDITORIUM WITH VIEW OF ORGAN GRILL. 1940. " '. . . balance between the various features and points of interest in the room.' " *Photo by Hedrich-Blessing*

The collaboration between Eliel and Eero Saarinen grew into a partnership when the two designers planned the Community House at Fenton, Michigan, in 1937. In the meantime, Eero had worked with Charles Eames on the revolutionary and now well-known molded-plywood chair design that was acclaimed when it was exhibited at the Museum of Modern Art.

Upon the completion of the Fenton plan, the partnership between father and son continued in the architectural office which they set up; in 1939 they joined with J. Robert F. Swanson to found the firm of Saarinen, Swanson, and Saarinen. It was maintained for eight years.

Father and son worked together in the firm Saarinen, Saarinen and Associates in Bloomfield Hills from 1947 to 1950. An architect who was intimately associated with the family and who worked in this new firm, said, "The father's advice was always respected by the son; on the other hand, Eero was always encouraged to advance his ideas by a very tolerant father."

From Buffalo, New York, came an opportunity of great importance in the careers of both Eliel and Eero Saarinen. The contract to design the Kleinhans Music Hall was signed in 1938. This was the first significant architectural project that came to Eliel Saarinen outside the

125 COLUMBUS, INDIANA. TABERNACLE CHURCH OF CHRIST (FIRST CHRISTIAN CHURCH). PULPIT, ALTAR, AND CHOIR STALL. 1940. Tapestry by Loja Saarinen 27 × 12 feet. *Photo by Hedrich-Blessing*

126 COLUMBUS, INDIANA. TABERNACLE CHURCH OF CHRIST (FIRST CHRISTIAN CHURCH). SUNKEN GARDEN WITH POOL. 1940. ". . . dispels the fear that a 'modern' building is necessarily cold and expressionless." *Photo by Hedrich-Blessing*

campus of Cranbrook during his residence in the United States and the first important and most successful opportunity for Eero to collaborate with his father. The design they created received wide recognition.

With the Buffalo firm of F. J. and W. A. Kidd as architects in charge of construction, the Saarinens developed the designs with detailed drawings and a model which showed with remarkable fidelity the building's exterior and interior. In view of the technical requirements of this concert hall, the conception was in itself as complicated as a musical instrument, molded completely by numerous techniques difficult to coordinate.

All the elements of the Kleinhans concert hall come together in a unified organism. Here, as in the Gothic cathedral, the building not only satisfies utilitarian requirements but also expresses the aesthetic purpose of the structure. It is one of the most satisfying examples of Eliel Saarinen's philosophy of design, enriched by Eero's contributions.

With the assistance of Stanley McCandless, lighting consultant, and Charles C. Potwin, acoustical adviser, the practical demands of the structure were met; the experts were so successful that the concert hall has frequently been lauded in words of highest praise by performing artists who could feel its excellence.

The large auditorium, which seats about three thousand, and the smaller one, with a capacity of about eight hundred, are models of the integration of architectural designing with technical considerations. Eliel Saarinen and his son arrived at a plan which, like a fine musical instrument, fulfills its mechanical purpose and which, again like a well-made instrument, is an honest expression in the art of design.

Eliel Saarinen himself made this comparison: "The shape of the violin has not derived from a preconceived style form. It has derived from and through its own function as a musical instrument and with distinct requirements as to the quality and carrying capacity of its sound, and as to how it is handled by the player. That is, the shape of the violin is based on both musical and human qualifications. And as a concert auditorium to its inmost nature is a musical instrument, its formation must derive accordingly."

Could it be this thought of the violin which gave the floor plan a shape resembling somewhat

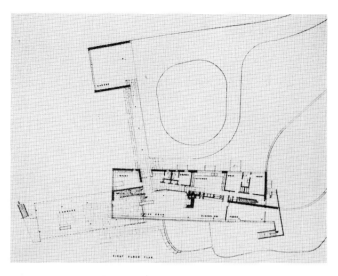

128 FORT WAYNE, INDIANA. A. C. WERMUTH HOUSE. SOUTH VIEW. 1941. "unification of a design, upon which both Eliel and Eero Saarinen worked . . . a common goal toward which both contribute a variety of concepts . . . a gradual process of amalgamation." *Photo by Askew*

127 FORT WAYNE, INDIANA. A. C. WERMUTH HOUSE. FIRST FLOOR PLAN. 1941. *Eero in collaboration with Eliel Saarinen, Architects*

129 FORT WAYNE, INDIANA. A. C. WERMUTH HOUSE, OUTDOOR LIVING ROOM. 1941. ". . . full appreciation of . . . topographical situation . . ." *Photo by Askew*

130 FORT WAYNE, INDIANA. A. C. WERMUTH HOUSE. LIVING ROOM. 1941. ". . . simple logic which makes for comfort and convenience." *Photo by Neuman*

that instrument? But, of course, the seating arrangement will also show immediately that the form was chosen in order to seat the largest number of people with the least waste of space. The auditoriums were designed to seat the audience so that each member might have a comfortable view of the stage.

The apparent proportions of the smaller music hall are increased by the reflecting pool, and, at the same time, charm is added to the setting of the building. The outer wall in this section is a good example of the elegance and warmth of detail that are characteristics of Eliel Saarinen's work.

In the interior of the auditoriums the Saarinens showed their ability to relate the proportions, colors, and textures to the spiritual expression of the building. There were, in these two halls, vital problems of function which needed

to be solved above all. Eliel said, "In order to satisfy the demands of the spiritual issue, there were many practical and technical requirements which were of basic significance.

"First, there were the acoustical requirements, which to a considerable degree determined the general form of the auditorium and the disposition of the stage, seats, and surfaces. Furthermore, these acoustical requirements decided much of the character and texture of the ceiling, walls, and floor covering, so as to ascertain satisfactory reverberation.

"Second, there was the problem of an adequate relationship between the musicians on the stage and the public in the auditorium proper. In this respect we do not mean particularly that practical matter of adequate sight from every chair, but even the psychological side of a pleasant participation in the performance.

"Third, there was the problem of shaping the auditorium so as to provide for possibilities of various and varying light effects according to the changing moments and accents, as the performance proceeds. This point the designers considered of particular importance, as the proposed double lighting with cold and warm color is essential in the bringing of forms and proportions to their full value and also in bringing the varying light effects into accord with corresponding variations of performance and intervals."

These and many more practical aspects were blended with aesthetic ones. Detailed consideration of all of them is stressed here because the manifold concerns of the designer can be completely understood only when there is, in the designer's own words, a full explanation of the possibilities which he allows and the limitations to which he submits himself. In the Kleinhans design the wealth of ideas that prompted the creators are stated in Eliel Saarinen's words and revealed in the finished structure. It is one of the outstanding examples of the art of Eliel and Eero Saarinen.

In the interior plan, color was used judiciously to produce the effect the designers wished to achieve. Eliel explained:

"The soft-blue fabric of the main auditorium is intended to bring a quiet scale of color to the room, together with the light-wood color of the walls and the light-gray color of the ceiling. This color combination of subdued character is apt still more to emphasize the strongly indicative lines of the auditorium design. Moreover, this color combination of subdued character is and will always be seen together with the varying and gradually rising and sinking effects of electric light in both warm and cold tones. Such being the case, it is obvious that the color selection of the auditorium and the study of the lighting problem have been worked out hand in hand with the auditorium design itself. And the color selection for the two auditoriums already settles to a certain degree the color key of the whole building throughout the various rooms."

Surrounded by ample space, rich in natural growth, the Kleinhans Music Hall offered an opportunity which, unfortunately, comes all too

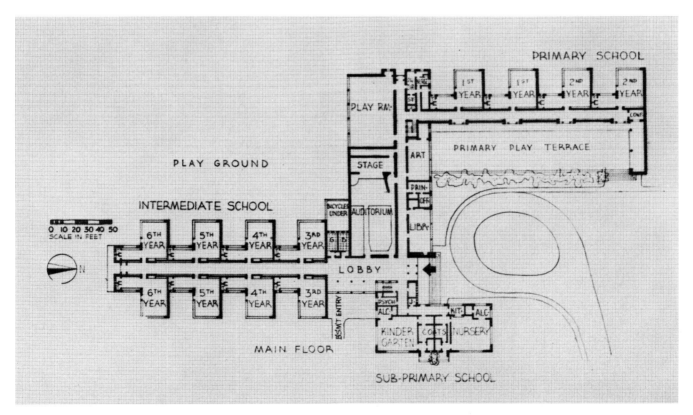

131 WINNETKA, ILLINOIS. CROW ISLAND SCHOOL. MAIN FLOOR PLAN. 1939. ". . . arranged to bring light and air into the various classrooms"

132 WINNETKA, ILLINOIS. CROW ISLAND SCHOOL. ELEVATION. 1939. ". . . to relieve the long, horizontal lines of the flat roofs, the chimney is designed to balance . . ." *Photo by Harold Nelson*

rarely in the life of a designer. The money available for this project gave sufficient freedom to the designers' imaginations. The liberal and willing spirit of the committee's request was one that encouraged the best design that the artists could conceive. The cooperation of capable and understanding colleagues supplied the technical features the building had to possess.

As a result, this gift to the people of Buffalo has been adjudged to be one of the works of art in contemporary architectural design. Joseph Hudnut, of Harvard, wrote: "If I had my way, every city in America should have a Kleinhans Music Hall, fitted like a garment to the idea of music as popular solace and enlightenment—an act of faith made express and visible."[6]

6. Joseph Hudnut, "Kleinhans Music Hall, Buffalo, N.Y.," *Architectural Form* 75 (July 1941): 41.

6

In 1940 the two designers combined their talents again in a project, which, like the Kleinhans Music Hall, offered them a unique opportunity to produce a building not restricted by a long list of limitations. A committee from Columbus, Indiana, came to Eliel Saarinen's studio and said: "We are asking you to build a church which will interpret the spirit of Christ and of the gospel and which will also promote these ideals and assure their perpetuation among us." With a generous donation from a member of this congregation, the committee enabled the Saarinens to produce their interpretation of the program as outlined by this statement.

On the ground floor plan, rectangular in shape,

133 WINNETKA, ILLINOIS. CROW ISLAND SCHOOL. 1939. ". . . small courts of flagstone walks and shrubs . . ."
Photo by Harold Nelson

the designers arranged the spaces of the building proper, flanking them with a series of classrooms, joined by a connecting bridge to the main structure. The bridge, supported by columns, contains two floors of the church school. At the center of the plan the pool complements the simple brick structures and the natural forms that surround the tabernacle.

Compared with the usual ecclesiastical building, the Columbus church contains a relatively small main auditorium because, in a study of the function of this church, the need for space for the many services the church would offer to the community was carefully considered. Because of this consideration, the building does not follow the traditional lines of a church structure; it meets the requirements of the congregation in a typical midwestern city of the twentieth century.

An examination of the exterior reveals the discipline of Eliel Saarinen's years of thought; analyses given to materials and their well-considered use produced a result that ought to dispel the fear expressed by many who insist that a "modern" building is necessarily cold and expressionless. The balanced masses, excellently supplied with relief in detail, are warm, inviting, and appropriate for their particular function.

The general horizontal feeling of the roof lines is given strength and variety by the upward movement of windows, elongated and effectively coordinated with the interior need for light, and is balanced by the tower which is one of the most striking of the designer's many studies of the horizontal mass in balanced unity with the vertical.

The appearance of the church interior gives a restful and responsive feeling to the visitor.

135 WINNETKA, ILLINOIS. CROW ISLAND SCHOOL. UNIT COURTYARD. 1939. ". . . so that the children at play would be attracted . . ." *Photo by Hedrich-Blessing*

134 WINNETKA, ILLINOIS. CROW ISLAND SCHOOL. DETAIL. 1939. ". . . [Lily Swann Saarinen's] animal sculptures . . . lend an intimate and charming aspect . . ." *Photo by Harold Nelson*

136 WINNETKA, ILLINOIS. CROW ISLAND SCHOOL. CLASSROOM. 1939. ". . . the architects were considerate of the welfare of the children . . ." *Photo by Hedrich-Blessing*

The altar, a simple, unadorned area, is given the eternal symbol of the cross, placed with calculated skill to the right of the pulpit. The tapestry above the choir stalls, woven by Loja Saarinen, balances the grill of the organ opposite.

Orderly in design, the church has no static symmetry. It has the advantage of variety. "We have not been concerned," said Eliel Saarinen, "with a symmetrical solution, believing that forced symmetry only creates artificial and sterile conditions. Really, in this design, symmetry was bound to be artificial, for the function of this church, in particular the function of the chancel, is asymmetrical in its nature. Our endeavor, therefore, has rather been to arrive at a good balance between the various features and points of interest in the room."

That the designers achieved this ambition is sensed by those who worship in the Tabernacle Church (now First Christian Church); the eyes of the audience turn naturally to the climax of the altar decoration and go, without interruption, from there to either the choir and the tapestry or to the pulpit. No columns interrupt this view, no ornately decorated areas of wall distract the attention.

Something of the simplicity and directness of the early Christian spirit is caught in this architecture. And it may be that only in a search for these fundamentals can the new ecclesiastical architecture be found.

In view of the comprehensive nature of the problem of church design for a modern community, the Tabernacle Church is one that dares

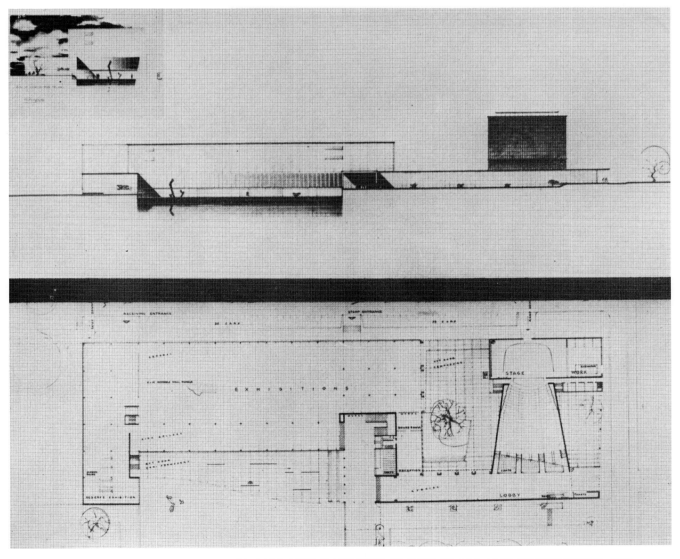

137 WASHINGTON, D.C. SMITHSONIAN ART GALLERY. FLOOR PLAN AND ELEVATION. 1939.

state its purpose and that ventures a new solution. How this solution was discovered, from the viewpoint of the nonfunctional or spiritual aspect, is expressed by the Reverend T. K. Smith: "There was no traditional architectural style that could be successfully employed to express our purpose. For generations the basic pattern of a church structure has remained practically unchanged. At best the recent designs have been recreations of traditional styles. None of these could fully express the grandeur and yet the simplicity of Christian faith unencumbered by human creeds and human symbolism. The only alternative was to find an architect whose creative genius would make possible the realization of such an expressive building. This

was accomplished when Eliel Saarinen consented to accept this assignment."[7]

Eliel Saarinen realized the dilemma of the designer who would conceive the structure of the Christian church in a contemporary form. Before he was invited to accept this commission he had frequently stated that because of the preconceptions and prejudices that usually exist when ecclesiastical architecture is considered, he would not design another church. Because he regarded the dilemma so seriously, the solution he and his son formulated is one that will stand as evidence of the progress we are making during

7. T. K. Smith, D.D., "Tabernacle Church of Christ," *Shane Quarterly* 4 (October 1943): 254.

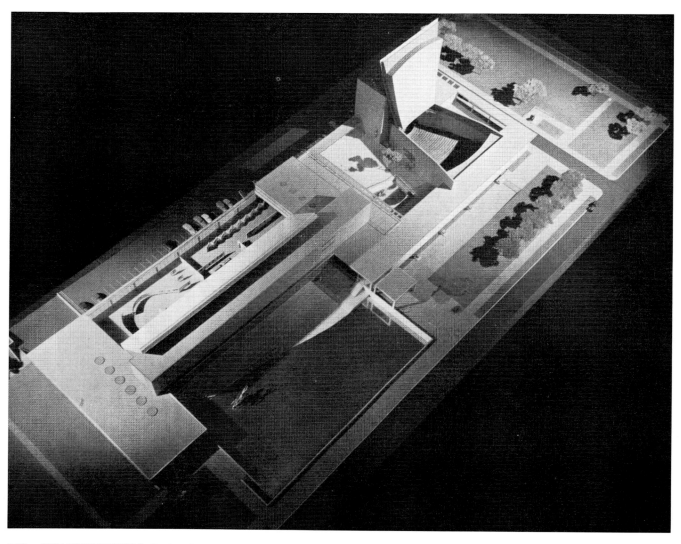

138 WASHINGTON, D.C. SMITHSONIAN ART GALLERY. MODEL. 1939. "'. . . remarkable clarity of composition in mass and a restraint and dignity of expression . . .'" *Photo by Askew*

139 WASHINGTON, D.C. SMITHSONIAN ART GALLERY. MODEL. FRONT ELEVATION. 1939. ". . . rad-ically departing from the column-consciousness of the public building . . ." *Photo by Askew*

140 WASHINGTON, D.C. SMITHSONIAN ART GALLERY. MODEL. REAR ELEVATION. 1939. ". . . a plan which would serve its purpose in the present . . . in future years by the addition of exhibition and storage space . . ." *Photo by Askew*

this century toward a community of opinion regarding the expressive forms of the Christian house of worship.[8]

7

Eliel Saarinen had devoted a considerable part of his career in Finland to designing domestic architecture. As we have seen, he designed the interiors, furniture, and appointments.

The homes that he designed were never small;

8. For such evidence, see Albert Christ-Janer and Mary Mix Foley, *Modern Church Architecture* (New York: McGraw-Hill Book Co., 1962).

he usually worked with a substantial budget. In fact, Eliel Saarinen was not often confined within meager limitations. In America he had been busy with the monumental and with only a few rather expensive residences.

"However, I was never so far distant from the problem of domestic architecture," said Eliel Saarinen, "as was the Beaux-Arts committee which presented to the students of architecture their first residential design problem. The stipulation had to do with designing a home for an exiled king, on the shores of the Mediterranean!"

His experience with the villas and country houses he had designed in Europe led Eliel Saarinen to anticipate many problems in the plan for

Kingswood. The dormitory space and the living quarters for the instructors gave him opportunity to fulfill the requirements of residential architecture.

When he began to design all the buildings on the Cranbrook campus as well as meet his instructional duties, he was fully occupied. He had no time for commissions that might have come from the field of domestic building. After he had completed most of the Cranbrook structures, the mark of the "builder of monuments" was on him.

"This is really not a healthy condition," Eliel Saarinen said, "because it requires a fresh mind, with a new viewpoint, to produce something fresh. I think it unwise to develop specialists in design, in general."

141 TANGLEWOOD, STOCKBRIDGE, MASSA-CHUSETTS. BERKSHIRE MUSIC CENTER. GENERAL LAYOUT. 1938. "These structures were to comprise the Berkshire Music Center"

142 TANGLEWOOD, STOCKBRIDGE, MASSACHUSETTS. BERKSHIRE MUSIC CENTER. MUSIC SHED. AERIAL VIEW. 1938. ". . . the concept which the architect and Koussevitsky formulated." *Photo by Babbitt*

During the time they were associated with J. Robert F. Swanson, and after he and Eero had set up an office, Eliel Saarinen carefully observed another of his principles about designing: an architectural office should not be a design factory. Only so much business should be accepted which would permit the maintenance of a high level of performance.

Because circumstances took him away from domestic architecture, Saarinen had not designed many residences in the United States excepting those at Cranbrook. The one presented here, the home of A. C. Wermuth, Fort Wayne, Indiana, was built in 1941 in collaboration with Eero. The son produced the plot plan and the elevation drawings and the father worked as an advisor.

The process of the unification of a design upon which both Eliel and Eero Saarinen worked had many variations, but, in general, there was a common goal toward which both contributed a variety of concepts. These ideas were discussed, the drawings of each examined, and a gradual process of amalgamation set in which produced the final scheme—in most cases an inseparable combination. Such harmonization would not be possible were it not for the fact that, in years of working together, the two designers became perfectly attuned to each other. Since both designers were strongly individual, neither was ever a secondary partner. The collaboration was possible only because father and son were in intellectual and spiritual accord. It was a rare friendship.

In the design of the Wermuth residence the collaborative process was relatively simple. It involved a rather small structure, and in the office only Eliel and Eero Saarinen worked upon it. The site for this house proved interesting, for it had an inviting view of wooded acres to the south.

The work of the Saarinens in domestic archi-

143 TANGLEWOOD, STOCKBRIDGE, MASSACHUSETTS. BERKSHIRE MUSIC CENTER. OPERA HOUSE. 1944. ". . . revealing the younger Saarinen's stricter functional approach." *Photo by Gottscho-Schleisner*

144 CRANBROOK ACADEMY OF ART. MUSEUM AND LIBRARY. SKETCH. 1940. ". . . intimate and effective use of sculpture and architecture as complementary art forms . . ."

tectural design is characterized by a clear logic that makes for comfort and convenience. There are no "house beautiful" effects. Because the plan is unostentatious, some examination is required before its thoughtful and direct quality reveals itself. The balanced proportion of the living-dining room is unified by a long span of windows, which open onto a ravine. The room is partially divided by the fireplace walls. The variation in the depth of this room, expanding in width into the living room where space is required for entertaining guests, is hospitable. The relationship between the maids' rooms and the work areas of the lower floor is convenient. Separated from the general household traffic, the library is located in an isolated area of the house, in privacy and quiet.

The second floor is a straightforward arrangement of sleeping quarters, with a sitting room and bedroom apartment on the west side above the terrace.

The interior is a paragon of restful simplicity. "I feel it ought to have a neutral quality," said Eliel Saarinen, "so that any sensible furniture can fit in."

The overall character of the structure was conditioned by the client's program; he asked for a house that would incorporate the best of the aspects he admired in the various Cranbrook houses on Academy Road.

8

With the extensive experience that Eliel Saarinen had gathered in the development of the schools of Cranbrook, it was not long before he was called to make plans for other educational institutions. The requests he received included the architectural plans not only for single school buildings but also for the development of college and university campuses. Many educators began to arrive at Cranbrook to ask the designer for counsel and aid.

In 1939 the board of education and the superintendent of the elementary school at Winnetka, Illinois, set out to find architects who could present plans for an institution devoted to an idealistic, but practicable, program of child training. Superintendent Carleton Washburne, an educator of broad experience and imagination, called upon a firm of young and progressive architects, Perkins, Wheeler, and Will, and asked them to draw up a plan for the school in collaboration with Eliel and Eero Saarinen, "a beautiful, practical architectural embodiment of an educational philosophy." The educational policy of this school, now a classic model, was a progressive one in which the child was accepted as a child and not as an adult's idea of what a child should be. Through scientific research the "park-school" plan was developed, an original scheme of laying out an area for training and recreational purposes. It was a broad and inclusive concept, one that attracted the creative forces which were finally to solve this problem and give the Illinois community one of the most forward-looking and attractive educational institutions in the United States.

The designs were created by Eliel and Eero Saarinen and the detailed execution was completed by Perkins, Wheeler, and Will. Eero's first wife, Lily Swann Saarinen, was commissioned to do the ceramic sculptures that were incorporated into the areas of the outer wall. These animal sculptures, by a most gifted ceramic sculptor, appeal to the children and lend an intimate and charming aspect to the simple, broad areas of brick construction.

The floor plan of the building is designed to bring an abundance of light and air into the classrooms. Primary and intermediate sections of the school are organized with small courts of flagstone walks and shrubs, contributing both to the sense of design and to the sense of spaciousness.

The brick walls carry large sections of glass to admit light into all rooms and hallways. The

145 CRANBROOK ACADEMY OF ART. ARCADE. SOUTH ELEVATION. 1940. Sculpture by Carl Milles and Marshall Fredericks. " '. . . has a special place in my estimation.' " *Photo by Hedrich-Blessing*

146 CRANBROOK ACADEMY OF ART. MUSEUM AND LIBRARY. ARCADE AND ORPHEUS GROUP. 1940. "Eliel Saarinen and Carl Milles . . . created a distinguished result . . ." *Photo by Hedrich-Blessing*

147 CRANBROOK ACADEMY OF ART. MUSEUM AND LIBRARY. UNITY OF DESIGN. 1940. "Balance with variety . . ." *Photo by Harvey Croze*

148 CRANBROOK ACADEMY OF ART. MUSEUM AND LIBRARY. NORTH VIEW. 1940. Orpheus group by Carl Milles; wildcats by Jussi Mäntymen. "The combination of Mankato stone and brick . . ." *Photo by Hedrich-Blessing*

149   CRANBROOK ACADEMY OF ART. LIBRARY. READING ROOM. 1940. *Photo by Hedrich-Blessing*

150   CRANBROOK ACADEMY OF ART. MUSEUM DESK. 1940. *Photo by Hedrich-Blessing*

chimney is designed to balance the long, horizontal lines of the flat roofs: a long, thin shaft elevated above the low and simple base. "We found that this area of form was necessary, a counterbalance to the underlying shape," said Eliel.

In every way that science could aid the designer in lighting, ventilation, and cleanliness, the architects provided for the welfare of the children who were to spend their hours of work and play in these rooms. The furniture, designed by Eero, and all the interior appointments in the building were scaled to children's needs; there are no overelaborate or forbidding refinements.

As Joseph Hudnut said: "The architects, I think, proceeded not *towards*, but *from*, the busy pattern of the society this building was to shelter. The design was shaped in their minds by the pressure and recessions of this society —of which it was to be both a consequence and a cause."[9] The architects saw the needs and the desires of children, and they were eminently

9. "Crow Island School, Winnetka, Illinois," with a comment by Joseph Hudnut, *Architectural Forum* 75 (August 1941): 85.

successful in expressing their realization. What they produced is already historic. It was awarded prize recognition by the American Institute of Architects in 1971, and Pipsan was at that time made an honorary member of the institute.

Of course, a building of this quality can be erected only if there is a demand for it. "Especial praise should be given a client when he evokes the best from a designer, and in the case of the Crow Island School the superintendent was wise and, therefore, unusual," said Eliel Saarinen.

9

"The design submitted by Eliel Saarinen," wrote Frederic A. Delano in the report of the jury for the Smithsonian Gallery of Art Commission, "is considered especially appropriate in its relation to the site. It offers a remarkable clarity of composition in mass and a restraint and dignity of expression which appear to the majority of the jury especially suitable for a building

151 CRANBROOK ACADEMY OF ART. SAARINEN RESIDENCE. COURTYARD VIEW. 1928. *Photo by Hedrich-Blessing*

152 CRANBROOK ACADEMY OF ART. SAARINEN RESIDENCE. LIVING ROOM. 1928. ". . . that distinctive quality which betokens the taste of the designer and his wife." *Photo by Hedrich-Blessing*

153 CRANBROOK ACADEMY OF ART. SAARINEN RESIDENCE. STUDIO. 1928. *Photo by Hedrich-Blessing*

154 CRANBROOK ACADEMY OF ART. SAARINEN RESIDENCE. STUDIO-LOUNGE. 1928. ". . . patterns characteristic of Loja Saarinen, usually geometric in shape and subdued in color . . ." *Photo by Hedrich-Blessing*

to be built on the Washington Mall. The building has the distinction which comes from a fine use of materials, and shows throughout a professional competency on the part of the designer which leads the jury to believe that he could be safely trusted with the execution of the work."[10]

This first prize was awarded to Saarinen, Swanson, and Saarinen in 1939, thirty-eight years after the elder Saarinen had completed his first design of a museum, the National Museum in Helsingfors. He had designed a number of galleries for science and art collections before he and his associates began work on the Smithsonian competition. The jury braved a storm of protest in recommending this plan, which departed radically from the column-consciousness of the public buildings of the nation's capital.

This was the first award since the time of Thomas Jefferson to be granted in open competition for the design of a public building of any importance in Washington, D.C. Because the prizes were given to established and recognized

10. "The Report of the Jury [Frederic A. Delano, John A. Holabird, Walter Gropius, George Howe, Henry R. Shepley]," *Architectural Forum* 71 (July 1939): 11. Design submitted by Eliel and Eero Saarinen, J. Robert F. Swanson, associate.

155 CRANBROOK ACADEMY OF ART. SAARINEN RESIDENCE. DINING ROOM. 1928. *Photo by Hedrich-Blessing*

architectural firms, it proved conclusively that there was little truth in the charge that an open competition would make for a blind choice of sensational, meretricious designs. The Smithsonian project established a precedent for future competitions for federal structures, although nothing of great note has yet resulted.

In considering the function of the museum that was to display and store the treasures of our national heritage, the designers proceeded to formulate a plan which would serve its purpose in the present and which, by careful forethought, could benefit in future years by the addition of exhibition rooms and storage space. The funds for the completion of this design were not granted by Congress, despite the efforts of Edward Bruce, the energetic and visionary head of the national arts program. After the untimely

death of Bruce the Smithsonian museum plan was set aside—permanently.

A superb scale model, made of metal, marble, and glass, was constructed by the designers. It presents the exterior as a direct revelation of its nature and content. It is placed in practical relationship to parking areas. The great exhibition area is lighted by a continuous window strip overlooking a court and the promenade on the borders of the pool situated near the main entrance of the museum.

The administration offices are located above the exhibition space. The theater, with its tapering auditorium and impressive stage house, complements the long, powerful line of the roof of the exhibition galleries.

The quality of this design, recognized by a distinguished jury, was never denied. A dozen

156 DESIGN. SAARINEN RESIDENCE. DINING ROOM. Fabrics by Loja Saarinen. Furniture by **Eliel Saarinen**.
Photo by Hedrich-Blessing

cities in other states erected functional civic buildings meanwhile; it is regrettable that Washington must bow to their architectural leadership.

In 1938 in collaboration with Sergei Koussevitzky, Eliel Saarinen designed the Music Pavilion for the Berkshire Symphonic Festival at Tanglewood, Massachusetts, the summer home of the Boston conductor's musical organization. The model of this plan shows the concert shell, the outdoor amphitheater, and the opera house, with a school and an inn for the students and visitors. These structures were to comprise the Berkshire Music Center.

The suggestions contained in the model were not carried out in detail. "But this is not a bad thing," said Eliel Saarinen, "because conditions change and a plan should not attempt to frustrate the forces of change. There must be flexibility—no rigid scheme—which will accommodate the requirements of the future."

In a general way the construction of the concert shell followed the design of the architects, though pillars were used within the auditorium in spite of Eliel Saarinen's opposition. The form of the structure, however, is in keeping with the plan he drew up, the basic idea in agreement with the concept he and Koussevitzky formulated.

Five years after the concert shell was completed, the designers made the drawings for the Opera Hall. This structure was developed with the simplest functioning construction. Charles C. Potwin and Stanley McCandless assisted. The practical qualities of this auditorium are "wellnigh perfect," according to Oliver Daniel, then musical director of the Columbia Broadcasting System. It is a rationally designed structure built at minimum cost and suitable for the needs of the center when the occasion calls for the production of small operas and chamber music recitals.

"We planned the auditorium so that its volume and shape required no sound-absorbing materials to obtain the proper reverberation time," said Eliel Saarinen. This was done through a scientific arrangement of exposed studs and the use of bituminous paving for the floors.

This is a building in which the hand of Eero Saarinen is plainly visible, revealing the younger partner's concern for a stricter engineering approach. That this method of construction produced the results desired by the architects is revealed in a comment made by an official of a broadcasting company: "One can credit the designers with having achieved next to the impossible."[11]

10

Eliel Saarinen began work on the design for the museum and library of the Cranbrook Academy of Art in 1940. As the final major addition to the academy, George G. Booth and Saarinen decided to build the structure which is the most monumental on the campus of the Cranbrook art center.

In preparation for the design of this exhibition hall and library the designer made a thorough study of museums by traveling in this country and in Europe to see the art galleries that had been acclaimed for possessing certain excellent features. But the most valuable information he received came from the industrial concerns which had experimented in lighting, ventilation, and air conditioning. When he had gathered a fund of material, he began to work on his plans for the Cranbrook Museum.

"My favorite building is always my next one," said Eliel Saarinen, "but the museum and library building at Cranbrook has a special place in my estimation."

In this structure Eliel Saarinen's sense of space, texture, and the relationships of shapes—the shapes enriched by the architectural ornament that makes his design distinctive—produced what may turn out to be his most memorable creation. It is the result of his lifelong search for form.

The function of the building is to display a collection of art objects against a quiet background and, in the library, to provide the student with a pleasant, well-lighted environment in which he may study. That it fulfills its function can be ascertained by even a casual glance at the building. It has been studied by architects from all over the world.

The exterior, though plain to the point of austerity, is a study in details of form, color, and texture. The combination of Mankato stone and

11. "Opera Shed," *Progressive Architecture* 28 (March 1947): 56.

brick shows the designer's ability to work with these mediums, with which he had thoroughly familiarized himself. Since 1931 he had employed the warm, delicately textured stone with the Wyandotte brick. Used at focal points and at the base level of the structure, the stone is sparingly ornamented with a motif which, though highly personal, is as universal in its quality as a geometric symbol.

"Frequently I am asked the meaning of these supposed symbols," said the designer. "Perhaps I am expected to answer that they are Finnish script; however, they are pure abstractions."

The relationship between the museum and library building and the older structures on the campus is sympathetic; harmony is produced by a coordination of proportions and the use of similar materials. When Joseph Hudnut was asked by the building committee of a large col-

lege whether it would be wise to continue in the established Gothic style he answered: "You need not build in a similar style to attain unity on this campus. A good design in proper scale will bring the harmony you desire." The Cranbrook Academy of Art campus is an excellent illustration of Hudnut's observation. Scale unifies those buildings; the result sets an example for the planning committees of the educational institutions who wish to employ a contemporary method of construction, incorporating the best of today's design and materials.

The association this building program fostered between Eliel Saarinen and Carl Milles has created a distinguished result. The pools, one with Tritons and the other with Orpheus figures, and the areas in and about the arcade displaying a variety of sculptures on pedestals, contain some of the best examples of the work of the Swedish sculptor. A more intimate and effective use, in recent times, of sculpture and architecture as complementary art forms would be difficult to discover. The spirit promoted by this collaboration is one that harks back to the Renaissance in Italy and France; Cranbrook is a distinctive architectural creation which, as Director Francis Henry Taylor of the Metropolitan Museum said during one of his visits in 1946, by combining an "inner peace and exterior comfort with its almost eighteenth century qualities of clarity and measure, is virtually unique in the world."

11

Because his study of museum function and design resulted in the distinguished central building of the Cranbrook complex, Eliel Saarinen was sought out by the building committee of the Edmundson Memorial Museum, since renamed the Des Moines Art Center. In 1944, in association with J. Robert F. Swanson and the Iowa firm of John Brooks and Elmer Borg, he presented the design that was subsequently built. The services of well-known designer Thomas Church were secured for the landscaping and Carl Milles was commissioned as sculptor. It was completed within five years. "Architect Eliel Saarinen has given Des Moines an art center which is fast becoming a source of pride to its

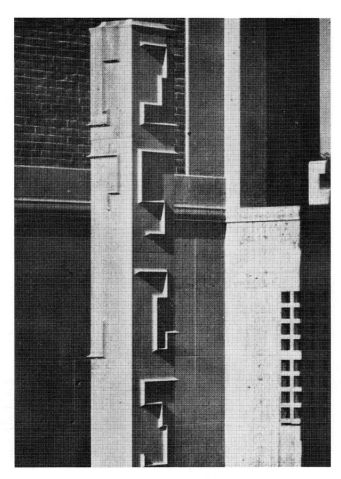

157 DESIGN. PILLAR FOR SCULPTURE. ". . . a creator of form." *Photo by Harvey Croze*

citizens," said a complimentary review of the completed structure.[12]

Within a year of its opening, the art center was recognized in the region as a vital institution which drew wide acclaim for its realistic, creative program; it offered art education services to children and a broad exhibition program to the general public. Harriet Coggeshall reported in *The Iowan*, May, 1953, "A beautiful building on top of one of Des Moines hills is the seat of an exciting venture in art which is drawing national attention. It is the home of the young, ambitious Des Moines Art Center. A low-lying structure of Wisconsin dolomite stone, the Center is the creation of Eliel Saarinen. It is already recognized as one of the outstanding examples of museum design.

"The Center folds naturally over the Greenwood Park hill. The only trace of formal landscaping is evident when the visitor passes through the building to the large reflecting pool terrace which contains the Carl Milles fountain sculpture, 'Pegasus.' An atmosphere of ease and hospitality dominates the interior. Visitors are invited to sit, browse, smoke or pursue their various interests among the manifold exhibitions which have brought over 325,000 visitors through the Center's doors since the opening, in June, 1948."

The change from "museum" to "art center" was significant; it indicated that the cold monumentality so frequently associated with the museum building would be replaced by warmth and comfort. Eliel Saarinen, in working out a new idea of museum form at Cranbrook, had the experience to oblige the wishes of the Iowa planning committee, which drew up a program with intelligence and taste. The result is dignified and pleasant, not stern or pompous. It invites.

The interior spaces are, consequently, as attractive as Eliel Saarinen ever created. In fact, this design is distinguished by his very personal quality which, present in all the Cranbrook buildings, marks it as perhaps the last which was not thoroughly amalgamated with Eero's. It has, consequently, a place of special importance in his long, productive career.

12. *Architectural Forum* (July 1949).

The quality of the art center's design reflects the aesthetic conviction Eliel Saarinen stated when, during his last decade, he reflected on his life experience: "Ornament represents the spirit of man in an abstract form. It transposes the rhythmic characteristics of time into a significative pattern of line, form, and color. It evolves from the simple toward the rich, from directness toward symbol. In this evolution, ornament assimilates new ideas, new thoughts, and new patterns, until by and by it embodies decorative interpretations of floral and faunal forms and of all that man feels, observes, enjoys, and likes to live with. But no matter how ornament develops, it always is—or should be—a translation of emotions with inner meaning behind the forms; it always is—or should be—an emotional play of forms with sincerity at the bottom; it always is —or should be—a product of true art."

The central exhibition wing relates to an integrated formal garden plan, and together they form a unit. All the galleries are subject to frequent changes; traveling exhibitions are shown during an active season's schedule. Most of the entry walls and those of the lounge are covered with rift-grain oak; the galleries, of course, are of plaster, monk's cloth panels, and sections of well-laid concrete block. The lighting in the galleries is a combination of cold cathode in coves and incandescent lamps, with the occasional introduction of natural light, which, as Saarinen found in working out his lighting problems at Cranbrook, makes a successful blend with the artificial.

A modest auditorium is located in the wing connecting the exhibition halls and the art school. Small concerts and lectures are presented in it. The art school area in a separate wing is housed in well-proportioned studios somewhat reminiscent of those in the Kingswood School.

The final cost of this structure, largely covered by the James D. Edmundson endowment, amounted to about $675,000; the art center is situated on land in the park donated by the city of Des Moines.

An addition, empathic and exquisite, was later designed by I. M. Pei. It compliments the Saarinen work and, in turn, is enriched by it.

12

Eliel Saarinen's Cranbrook buildings had, by the mid-1940s, attracted national attention. One of those who came in search of a new plan and contemporary designs was President Henry Gadd Harmon of Drake University, in Des Moines, Iowa. Aware of the work the firm was doing for the Edmundson Museum, President Harmon requested such quality of design for his campus. In talking with Eliel Saarinen he said, "I know that a college president must raise money; I am one who enjoys it." His vigorous support presented the firm with the possibility of erecting excellent buildings on his needy campus.

The first construction erected from the plans for a greatly enlarged new campus was the distinctive Science and Pharmacy Building, completed by Saarinen, Swanson, and Saarinen and published thoroughly in *Progressive Architecture*, where these units were acclaimed as "remarkably successful and beautiful examples of integrated design." Eero's influence in the design of this building is evident; the son's ideas were beginning to take ever more visible form. Eliel Saarinen saw this structure completed before his death.

It was remarkable that an institution so hard pressed for endowment funds would commission and accept "such unpretentious architecture, not only to construct these two initial units but also to base the entire future program around the same design thesis. Behind this straightforward approach is Drake's enlightened policy of using its funds to the limit in making education available to all applicants, and not spending a cent on the costly, the nonproductive, or the showy."

"It is always a pleasure," continued the reviewer, "to report the final fillip of successful architecture—that the clients are pleased."[13]

The head of the biology department, one of those who would be served daily by the efficiency of this design, said, "It was in the planning of the unified function that the architects showed their particular skill. The buildings were connected by an overhead pass that allows free

13. *Progressive Architecture,* November 1950, pp. 66 ff.

access; but the unification is affected by more than this. One has a feeling that, while the two buildings are separate, they definitely are a unit —that one is the adjunct of the other, that neither is just tacked on. The subtleties of this functional unification are difficult to describe and were achieved through the concept of the architect." Eliel Saarinen was particularly delighted by this evaluation from a faculty member. "I work for him," he said.

Eliel Saarinen always responded to such challenges. Time and again he showed his idealism, natural for one of his convictions, in the way he greeted a sound program and a client of quality. Money was not his major concern. He always "traveled first class" because he took it for granted that he would be rewarded for work well done.

He could be a designer on a grand scale and yet be considerate of the low-budget project. Especially during his last years Eliel Saarinen

158 DESIGN. IRON GATE. *Photo by Hedrich-Blessing*

was altogether devoted to what he believed to be of true value.

Various school and college projects, stemming in many instances from the original firm of Saarinen, Swanson, and Saarinen, were completed in the offices of Eliel and Eero Saarinen and their associates, one of whom was Joseph N. Lacy. For example, a campus plan and some dormitories for women were designed for Antioch College, Yellow Springs, Ohio. The first units of a sizable plan were completed by 1949, a product of the united effort of the Saarinen firm, father and son, in association with Max G. Mercer, the Ohio associate architect. Dan Kiley, who frequently worked with Eero, was the landscape designer.

The campus plan included a dining hall, a library, theater arts building, and dormitories discriminatingly arranged around the towered Antioch Hall.

The three-story women's dormitory with its simple facade was flanked by a sunken court, which extended along the main lounge on the west side of the building. Arranged in a series of units, it accommodated 110 students. In addition to the main lounge it also contained social rooms for 30 students in each unit, three apartments for faculty members, and large areas of storage rooms.

This is another illustration of the degree of amalgamation with the character of his talented son which evolved at the end of Eliel Saarinen's career. In this dormitory, for example, the frame of reinforced concrete, the strict interior surfaces of brick, painted plaster, and natural birch, and above all the fenestration, in simple bands wrapped around the building, show the design quality of Eero's hand.

The Antioch College campus, then, reveals how difficult it is today to make a distinct line of separation between the work of Eliel and Eero, especially during the years 1948–50. While Christ Church Lutheran in Minneapolis is obviously related to the earlier Tabernacle Church (First Christian) in Columbus, Indiana, and must be regarded therefore as chiefly the work of Eliel Saarinen, the dormitory on this Ohio campus is more in Eero's style.

13

"Eliel and I got the call from officials of General Motors in December, 1944, to meet with them to discuss the Technical Center," Robert Swanson remembers. For many years the General Motors executives had aimed to make their company the leader of technological research. With the expectation of continuing their contributions to technological progress at an accelerated rate, they contemplated a vast center that could house almost five thousand scientists, engineers, designers, and technicians and their supporting personnel.

This complex of buildings, their program proposed, would be furnished with every conceivable type of tool and testing device; working conditions would be the best. "A campus-like atmosphere is sought deliberately so that these surroundings will stimulate creative thinking and excellent work," the plan envisioned.

"Here in the Technical Center," Charles F. Kettering promised when he spoke on the day of its dedication, over a decade after Eliel Saarinen first heard of its conception, "we now have a place where we can make an indefinite number of practice shots; the only time we don't want to fail is the last time we try."

All through the 1920s and 1930s Eliel Saarinen and Robert Swanson had been associated in various projects. "The first contract for the G.M. design was therefore in our joint names, Saarinen and Swanson. After developing an initial scheme, which the corporation's committee thought highly possible, we were given the go-ahead," Swanson has said.

Gathering the data and coordinating the evolving program for such an undertaking was an imposing task; months of fact-finding and planning were invested by the architectural firm.

The plot plan involved a flat area, a large expanse of land in Warren, Michigan, to the north of Detroit. In the first conceptions, Eliel Saarinen and Robert Swanson projected a scheme involving efficient parking and traffic patterns; the structures were adaptable to permit expansion. These concepts were dramatically rendered by the brilliant technician, Hugh Ferriss, whose drawing ability was renowned.

In 1945, the Ferriss renderings were ready for examination. They were elegant. Each showed a particular expanse of the tremendous project, from the overall view of the campus to a detail of a monumental, sculptured, cantilevered, covered walkway.

"I then managed to persuade Eero, on the strength of this large contract to come back to Bloomfield Hills," Swanson recalls. "During the war he worked with the Office of Strategic Services, in Washington, D.C." Eero returned; under the firm's name of Saarinen, Swanson, and Saarinen, the search for program solution went forward.

The first plan was not so strict, so Miesian, as the one that was built. The alteration resulted when Eero's influence became dominant, after the firm of Saarinen and Saarinen took over the job in 1947. A clear illustration of the change from the curvilinear to the straight line may be seen in the Dynamometer Building, a structure designed for testing engines. It became so evidently Mies-influenced that it would have been harmonious among the buildings of the Illinois Institute of Technology; it is more evidence of the respect Eero showed, over the years, for the style of the renowned German architect who had been brought to the United States in 1936 by President Henry T. Heald, of IIT, to design its new Chicago campus.

In the early stages of planning the free-form lake was envisioned by Eliel Saarinen and his associates. The use of a curving, soaring roof for the main research building contributed an additional quality of unusual distinction. Although the original design was strongly approved, the need for retrenchment and simplicity became irresistible after a long strike had clouded the economic future and bids had become too high for such designs.

All in all, only the first concept is the work of Eliel Saarinen, as shown here in the Ferriss renderings of his plan. "Upon the resumption of full-time work on the G.M. design in September, 1948," said Robert Swanson, "it was re-shaped by Eero, until the form of what was built finally emerged." Kevin Roche, who worked for Eliel Saarinen briefly before 1950, recalls, "General Motors Technical Center was almost completely redesigned by Eero with very little participation from Eliel, as I remember." After that date the dynamic power of the younger man asserted itself naturally in the firm established by the Saarinens. This development was not resisted by Eliel; in fact, he was proud of his son's achievement. And, in return, Eero was a respectful son, always showing his obvious regard for the opinions of his wise senior partner. Firm member Joseph N. Lacy recalls that although the final design of the G. M. Center bears Eero's indelible mark, Eero, while he was designing it, spent long hours in consultation with his father. Eliel was thus involved on a day by day basis as critic and collaborator.

"Except for a brief excursion into sculpture," Eero once reflected, after Eliel's death, "it never occurred to me to do anything but to follow in my father's footsteps and to become an architect. As his partner, I often contributed technical solutions and plans, but only within the concept he created. A better name for architect is form-giver and until his death in 1950, when I started to create my own form, I worked with the form of my father." Hence, the complete creation of the Technical Center, in 1956, was necessarily Eero's; he thus evolved, in this project, from the young partner to the brilliantly versatile architect who, in a brief time, made his mark.

His mature independence at the crowning point of his life, is stated exactly by him about two years before his untimely death, "My father, Eliel Saarinen, was a fine architect and a leader of his generation. He has been given his own deserved recognition. I shall be grateful if my efforts are successful. If they are, I would prefer to be recognized for my own success."

Eliel, ever loyal, understood; and he would have been prouder than anyone to have seen what Eero attained.

14

A year after World War II, William A. Buege, a young veteran and new pastor of the Christ Church Lutheran, Minneapolis, Minnesota, came to visit Eliel Saarinen in his studio on Academy Road. Upon reentering the life of a community church pastorate, he had decided to aim high; he would build the Lord's house in renewed faith and form.

"When we undertook the project of building a new church, neither I nor the congregation were acquainted with the field of modern architecture. In fact, I had seen only the more grotesque examples, which were enough to frighten one even from contemplating such a design for spiritual purposes. But we did come to feel that only a contemporary approach would have relevance in an effort to interpret our message to the present age. Our Gospel is as honest as it is simple, and we felt that the building should express these qualities. This led us to dissatisfaction with a Gothic design which had already been prepared for Christ Church before I took up my pastorate there.

"Looking back, I find it difficult to explain what moved me to this search for honest building and how I happened to think of going to the best architect to design our church. I recall that I did seek the advice of Prof. Roy Jones, the head of the architecture school of the University of Minnesota. He suggested that I visit a number of architects, especially Eliel Saarinen, then head of the Cranbrook Academy of Art. Through a good friend I was advised to look into what had been done in the Scandinavian countries, particularly Finland. Fortunately, this limited the choice of men greatly, almost exclusively to Saarinen. We looked for the best and by God's guidance were led to Saarinen. Those who do not believe in God and his guidance would call it luck.

"I cannot say today that I went to Bloomfield Hills, Michigan fully acquainted with the meaning of my mission. And I cannot say—as I would like to—that I knew the reputation of this world-famous man whom I was going to ask to consider our problem. No, I can only remember, with embarrassment, the questions I did ask and and the suggestions I made as we discussed the nature of our goal. My own education began after Eliel Saarinen accepted our commission and began to educate me and our church officers. It was, for all of us, a beginning.

"Why did he accept this challenge? I can tell you very simply. Eliel Saarinen consented to create our design—for very little money—because we gave him a program which, he said,

compelled him to create it. In simple terms what we said was this:

"'We want a house of worship reflecting our faith in our day and in our way. We want to praise God with our own hearts and hands.'

"Eliel Saarinen began to question us about our needs; the incubation period when the design took shape in his mind brought us into close communion with one another. It was a most rewarding association because I learned to know the greatest and humblest man that I have ever met. I am still able to draw most heavily on that association for understanding.

"At the end of the year, Eliel Saarinen was truly a member of our congregation. More than that, he was a teacher of us all and I can see why he used to say, 'An architect must first of all be an educator.' To further our education, we called in a competent theologian to present the history and development of church architecture so that the congregation could know that the presently accepted forms were not designs of God nor the only forms in which the church had worshipped. When Saarinen's prospectuses were ready, we used an entire week in presenting them to the congregation. I believe that these studies were important in opening the minds of the congregation to acceptance of an entirely new church design.

"When the church was built, it fulfilled our requirements more perfectly than we could ever have hoped or dreamed and more perfectly than I have ever seen anywhere else. Moreover, I believe that our church would have been good at any time in history, if this type of expression had been possible with the materials then to be had. Through its basic floor plan our church ties in firmly with the churches of all time, because ours and all others must meet certain liturgical requirements. It is the superstructure that expresses our life today. Church design must always have very firm roots in the past; otherwise it is merely an aberration.

"This church is a symbol of our faith; all of us feel that this is so and we thank the day when we were given the inspiration thus to express the best in us."

Eliel Saarinen, in consultation with Eero, conceived Christ Church as the setting against which the liturgical drama unfolds. Aurally, it was con-

159 SILVERWARE. 1929. *Photo by C.A.A.*

160 SILVERWARE. 1929. *Photo by C.A.A.*

161 DESIGN. BONBON DISH. BRASS. *Photo by C.A.A.*

162 DESIGN. FRUIT BOWL. BRASS. *Photo by C.A.A.*

163 DESIGN. BONBON DISH. BRASS. *Photo by C.A.A.*

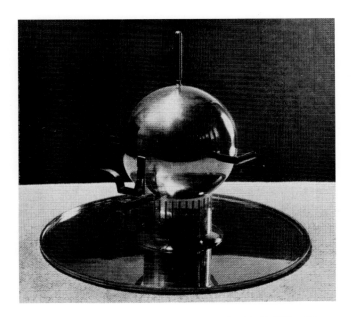

164 DESIGN. TEA URN. SILVER-PLATED. *Photo by C.A.A.*

119

ceived as an instrument for the projection of the Word of God and the ritual of music.

Because he felt that nothing should compete with the visible rite for the attention of the worshipper, the designer reduced the interior of the church to a background of unadorned simplicity, brought into brilliant focus by the use of lighting as a basic element of design. As acoustics are important to the apperception of both musical liturgy and sermon, the control of sound has been made the organizing factor through which most major and many minor elements of this church take their shape. Here Eero's concern and ability are revealed, too.

The result is a structure without precedent in ecclesiastical architecture. Christ Church achieves a rare beauty, giving no hint of the practical and infinitely painstaking scientific calculations upon which it is based. This church is proof of one of the more telling arguments for modern architecture: that only new forms can take full advantage of recent developments in acoustics, lighting, and other basic building sciences—and that these new forms can be as compelling as the forms they supersede.

The traditional styles, so sentimentally appealing to most congregations, were actually based on quite primitive concepts of sensory phenomena.

Today, in our smaller churches and with our changed concept of a religious service, the acoustical effect of borrowed Gothic can be distinctly unpleasant. At best, it takes no advantage of the superior potential of our age.

Christ Church, dedicated to a more intimate worship and to a Protestant concept of visibility and audibility, offers a whole solution. The basic structural system of this church is an extremely simple one: merely a steel frame enclosed by stone and brick walls, the latter exposed on the interior as well as the exterior. But the organization of these elements to achieve the acoustical and visual goal is a more complicated matter.

The major instrument of sound control is the shape of the building itself. Since sound waves reverberate back and forth between parallel surfaces, such surfaces have been avoided in the design. The flat ceiling, hung from a roof of steel decking, is canted slightly downward from side to side, thus presenting a surface that is not parallel to the floor. The north wall of the church is splayed out from front to rear, angling away from the straight south wall at the opposite end. Toward the front of the church, this north wall melts into the chancel wall as a gentle, continuous curve, thereby eliminating the right-angle meeting of wall surfaces that is ordinarily a focal point for echoes.

In addition to the shape of the church and the tilt and angle of surface details, the materials used in the interior have been chosen for their acoustical properties. They apply the principle that to provide clear tones without reverberation, a sound-reflective surface should be opposed by a sound-absorbent one. The hard floor and hard wooden surfaces of the pews are opposed by a suspended ceiling of perforated acoustic tile, backed at strategic areas by two inches of insulation. The solid brick south wall of the nave is opposed by the north wall, patterned with open brickwork repetitively splayed in and out from the wall line. The open space thus created behind the brickwork is backed by sound-absorbent material.

Because of Saarinen's concern for sound control, starting with the basic shape of the building and extending to minor details, the acoustics of Christ Church are probably the finest of any religious building in the United States. The tone and clarity of music within it is incomparable. Although not small—it seats 600—every syllable spoken by the minister is as clearly audible in the last row as it is in the front of the church. In effect, the congregation is "within" the service, at its acoustical center, rather than being merely at a crossover point in a path of reverberating sound.

The illumination of the church has been given equally conscientious attention. The only two sources of daylight are the glass walls of the side aisles and a narrow, vertical window strip lighting the chancel. The main area of the nave has no windows at all. However, because interior surfaces are of subdued coloring, this limited amount of daylight is reflected rather than absorbed, providing a soft yet ample illumination throughout the church, intensifying to radiant whiteness at the chancel.

Christ Church Lutheran, dedicated in 1949, was constructed for the remarkably modest sum of $300,000. Exposed brickwork eliminates the cost of surface finishes on this simple structure.

The double use of some spaces, such as the narthex and subsidiary chapel, further shrinks the costs. Even the seating arrangement in the nave is an economy. By continuing the pews without break into the aisles, the interior space has been utilized to its full seating capacity.

Christ Church thus represents economy as the result of painstaking planning, rather than reduced quality. The design as a whole achieves a memorable harmony and beauty. Its effect is perhaps best exemplified by the comment of a nonbeliever who visited this church. "I am not a Christian. But if I have ever felt like getting down on my knees, it has been here."

The effect of light, which had continued to interest Eliel Saarinen after his investigation of the problem in the galleries of the Cranbrook Museum of Art and in his design of Christ Church, Minneapolis, also absorbed him when he drew his plan for the Stephens College chapel. This is no doubt the final work of his hand; Eero did not participate in the development of these drawings which were completed during 1949–50.

Five years earlier, President James Madison Wood of Stephens College, Columbia, Missouri, had come to Cranbrook to appeal to Eliel Saarinen for help in expressing what Wood hoped would be the very spirit of interdenominational, personal worship. He expressed this simply, "I have always dreamed of building a small chapel in which every Stephens girl could find a quiet and private moment of spiritual comfort." When they met in his studio, the architect and Mr. Wood were united in the purpose; they enjoyed the mutual effort expended in forming the design.

The light, Mr. Wood felt, should be mysterious. It should descend from above; the outer world should be remote. Even if the chapel were full, each occupant should feel alone.

Eliel Saarinen delighted in this work. He spent hours planning it and rendering it. In fact, it was his last completed drawing for an architectural project. Unfortunately, it remained only a project, much to his and Mr. Wood's distress. The money was difficult to raise; the contractor's bids were high. The drawing might be regarded as a memorial for both the aging college president and the architect. Later, in 1957, a chapel was dedicated at Stephens College; it was Eero's.

15

Premier Urko Kekkonen, speaking at Eliel Saarinen's memorial service when his wife and son returned his ashes to his native land, spoke eloquently of Finland's affection and esteem for the renowned architect: "We pay tribute to the memory of Eliel Saarinen. His name in the field of architecture has become a concept.

"Style is the way of expression of a certain time. What is the style of Eliel Saarinen, that noble style of architecture that is known by all the world? It is an expression of the modern age in architecture. It is also the Finnish way of expression in architecture. But Eliel Saarinen's style is far greater; it cannot be tied by the fetters of passing time any more than it can be geographically restricted. Eliel Saarinen's style embraces parts of the best of all times. It has harmony that dates from the expression of bygone time; it has values that will be preserved by the generations to come. Eliel Saarinen's architectural art has grown far outside the national boundaries of Finland; it is owned by all the world. In the true sense of the word, it is the *style* of Eliel Saarinen.

"To the Finnish people, the significance of Eliel Saarinen is not limited to his architectural merits only. His significance to his people has been also more general. After he had moved outside its boundaries, he, with his architect's pen, inscribed the name of his native country, making it well known in the world. He always stressed his Finnish origin. His attachment to his country is touchingly witnessed by the fact that according to his wishes he was buried in the soil of his native land.

"To the memory of a son who has accomplished such an unforgettable life's work and made his country's name well known throughout the world, the Finnish people and the Finnish government present their respectful thanks.

"The present generation and the future Finnish generations will cherish the name of Eliel Saarinen with grateful hearts."

Alvar Aalto added his professional tribute, "Eliel Saarinen's life's work embraces an entire cultural epoch in our history. During that time, Finnish architecture blossomed simultaneously with the ripening of Finnish prose literature at the same time when music, poetry, and the fine arts reached their golden age. It was Eliel Saarinen who brought the exceptionally powerful contribution of architecture to this culmination of our culture.

"The creative geniuses of the epoch, among whom Eliel Saarinen had the leading position, created L'Art Nouveau-Jugend, which had developed on the Continent, adding the special Finnish feature. In Eliel Saarinen's works, this particular quality found distinctive expression. In the Finnish pavilion, which he built in 1900, Finland was for the first time presented on the Continent to become an influence on other countries. And from the culturally rich period at the beginning of the century, Finland had two parallel languages which had international influence: architecture and music. Eliel Saarinen, with Jean Sibelius, became the ambassador of his people.

"Eliel Saarinen as a city builder," Alvar Aalto continued, "was the first great Finnish 'urbanist.' He was the first who saw the problem of Helsinki in all its extensiveness; through him routine growth developed into city-planning that was conscious of its aims. Eliel Saarinen's greater Helsinki plans, as well as several of his other town plans, have been the incentive to the truly organic planning of communities, even to regional planning.

"Eliel Saarinen's architecture, too," Alvar Aalto concluded, "developed consistently from its pioneering stage; its development may be followed building by building. Most of these buildings today stand on foreign land, as he had moved his creative activities to the other side of the ocean. There, in the United States, he attained the fame which is to our eternal credit; therefore, Finland pays homage to this native son who is acclaimed also by the whole world."

LATE WORKS AND PROJECTS

LIKE MANY ARCHITECTS of his time, Eliel Saarinen was offered an unusual number of opportunities in design after 1944. The following plans were developed while he was senior partner in the firm of Saarinen, Swanson, and Saarinen or, after the spring of 1947, in the offices of Saarinen, Saarinen, and Associates. Two of the designs shown here, the Des Moines Art Center, Des Moines, Iowa, and Christ Church Lutheran, Minneapolis, Minnesota, were completed by 1949. This work is typical of the late creations of Eliel Saarinen.

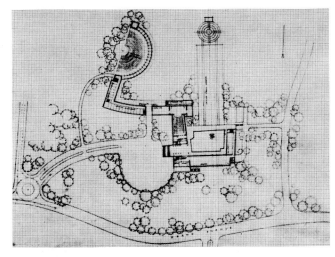

165 DES MOINES, IOWA. EDMUNDSON MEMORIAL MUSEUM. FIRST SCHEME. COMPREHENSIVE LAYOUT WITH THEATER AND OUTDOOR AMPHITHEATER. 1944

166 DES MOINES, IOWA. EDMUNDSON MEMORIAL MUSEUM. ART CENTER BASED UPON ORIGINAL SCHEME. 1944. *Sketch by Eliel Saarinen*

167 DES MOINES, IOWA. EDMUNDSON MEMORIAL MUSEUM. INSIDE COURT WITH POOL. 1944.
Sketch by Eliel Saarinen

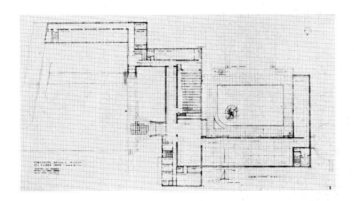

168 DES MOINES, IOWA. EDMUNDSON MEMO-RIAL MUSEUM. MAIN FLOOR PLAN OF AC-CEPTED DESIGN. 1944

169 DES MOINES, IOWA. EDMUNDSON MEMORIAL MUSEUM. 1944. *Rendering by Barr.*

170 DES MOINES, IOWA. DES MOINES ART CENTER. ENTRANCE. 1948. *Photo by Hedrich-Blessing*

171 DES MOINES, IOWA. DES MOINES ART CENTER. REFECTING POOL. 1948. *Photo by Hedrich-Blessing*

172 DES MOINES, IOWA. DES MOINES ART CENTER. "PEGASUS," BY CARL MILLES. *Photo by Tyler Studios*

173 DES MOINES, IOWA. DES MOINES ART CENTER. ENTRANCE GALLERY. 1948. *Photo by Hedrich-Blessing*

174 DETROIT, MICHIGAN. GENERAL MOTORS TECHNICAL CENTER. AERIAL VIEW. 1945. *Rendering by Ferriss. G.M. Photo*

175 DETROIT, MICHIGAN. GENERAL MOTORS TECHNICAL CENTER. AERIAL VIEW. ADVANCED ENGINEERING BUILDING. 1945. *Rendering by Ferriss. G.M. Photo*

176 DETROIT, MICHIGAN. GENERAL MOTORS TECHNICAL CENTER. AERIAL VIEW. RESEARCH BUILDING. 1945. *Rendering by Ferriss. G.M. Photo*

177 DETROIT, MICHIGAN. GENERAL MOTORS TECHNICAL CENTER. CANTILEVERED COVERED WALKWAY. 1945. *G.M. Photo*

178 DETROIT, MICHIGAN. GENERAL MOTORS TECHNICAL CENTER. ADMINSTRATION BUILDING. MAIN ENTRANCE. 1945. *Rendering by Ferriss. G.M. Photo*

179 DETROIT, MICHIGAN. GENERAL MOTORS TECHNICAL CENTER. INSIDE TERRACE OF ADMIN- ISTRATION BUILDING. 1945. *Rendering by Ferriss. G.M. Photo*

180 YELLOW SPRINGS, OHIO. ANTIOCH COLLEGE. AERIAL VIEW. CAMPUS PLAN. 1945

181 YELLOW SPRINGS, OHIO. ANTIOCH COLLEGE. LIBRARY. 1945. *Rendering by Barr*

182 YELLOW SPRINGS, OHIO. ANTIOCH COLLEGE. THEATER. 1945. *Rendering by Barr*

183 YELLOW SPRINGS, OHIO. ANTIOCH COLLEGE. DORMITORY. 1945. *Rendering by Fletcher*

x

130

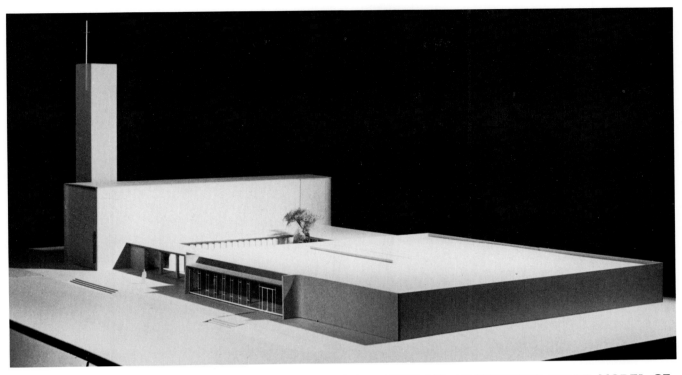

184 MINNEAPOLIS, MINNESOTA. CHRIST CHURCH LUTHERAN. ARCHITECT'S SCALE MODEL OF CHURCH AND EDUCATION BUILDING. 1949

185 MINNEAPOLIS, MINNESOTA. CHRIST CHURCH LUTHERAN. EXTERIOR AND DETAIL OF SCULPTURE. 1949. *Photo by Stalvig*

186 MINNEAPOLIS, MINNESOTA. CHRIST
CHURCH LUTHERAN. INTERIOR. 1949

187 MINNEAPOLIS, MINNESOTA. CHRIST
CHURCH LUTHERAN. 1949. *Photo by George
Miles Ryan*

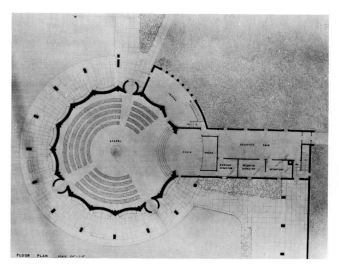

188 COLUMBIA, MISSOURI. STEPHENS COL-
LEGE CHAPEL. PLAN. 1947

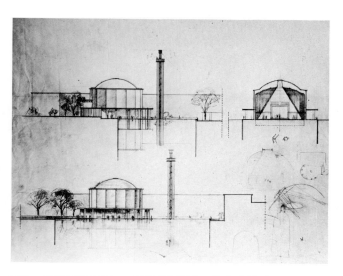

189 COLUMBIA, MISSOURI. STEPHENS COL-
LEGE CHAPEL. SKETCHES, ELEVATIONS,
SECTION. 1947

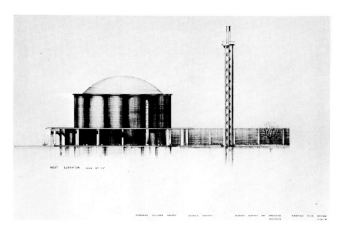

190 COLUMBIA, MISSOURI. STEPHENS COL-
LEGE CHAPEL. WEST ELEVATION. 1947

191 COLUMBIA, MISSOURI. STEPHENS COL-
LEGE CHAPEL. INTERIOR. 1947

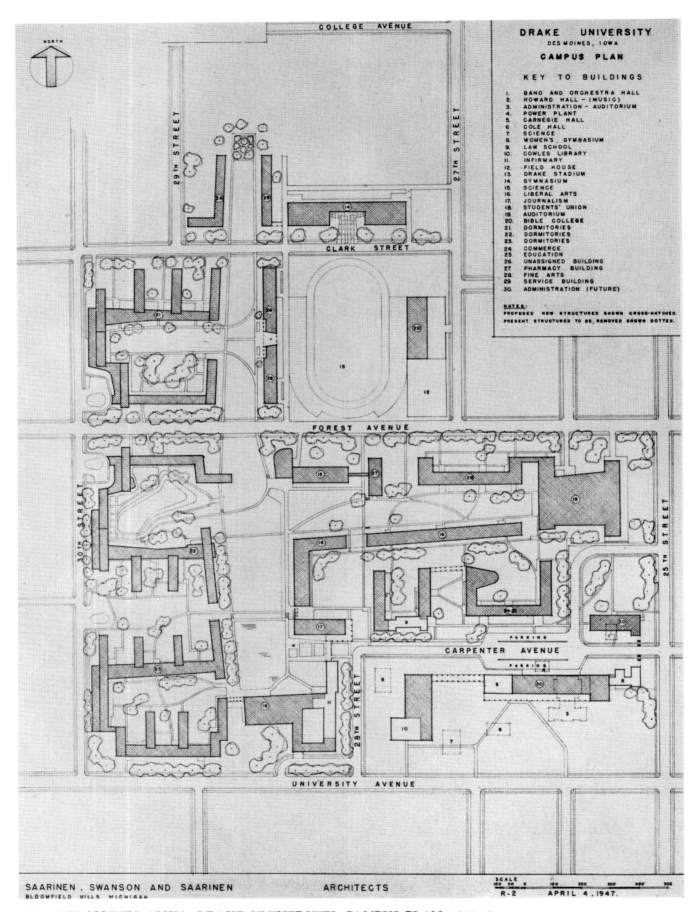

SAARINEN, SWANSON AND SAARINEN   ARCHITECTS
BLOOMFIELD HILLS MICHIGAN

SCALE
R-2   APRIL 4, 1947.

192 DES MOINES, IOWA. DRAKE UNIVERSITY. CAMPUS PLAN. 1946–47

English usage for place names in this text has attempted to follow the historical pattern. Place names mentioned prior to settlement of national boundaries after World War I are therefore Swedish. More recent allusions, particularly to Helsinki (Swedish: Helsingfors), are given the Finnish form.

1873 August 20 Gottlieb Eliel Saarinen born to Juho and Selma Broms Saarinen in Rantasalmi, Finland

1875 Moved with his family to Liisilä, Ingermanland, Russia, where his father was a pastor of the Lutheran church

1877 Moved with his family to Spankkova, also in Ingermanland

1883 Began visiting at L'Hermitage Museum in St. Petersburg, where he became acquainted with the great masters

1883 Entered the Klassillinenlyseo, a secondary school in Viborg, Finland

1889 Transferred to the Realyceum, a secondary school in Tammerfors, Finland

1893 Gathered folklore in Ingermanland during his summer vacation

1893–97 Simultaneously studied painting at the University of Helsingfors and architecture at Polytekniska Institutet in Helsingfors

1896 December 10 While still in school, established an architectural firm in Helsingfors with two classmates, Herman Gesellius and Armas Lindgren

1897 Was graduated from Polytekniska Institutet in Helsingfors, from which he received a traveling scholarship

1899 Married Mathilda Gyldén. Although the exact length of the marriage is uncertain, it was fairly short-lived. Date of divorce may have been 1902 or 1903. Mathilda later married Herman Gesellius, possibly in 1903

1899–1900 Designed and supervised the building of the Finnish Pavilion for the Exposition Universelle Internationale in 1900 in Paris and became acquainted during his stay there with artists of many countries; studied painting under Eugène Carrière at the Académie Moderne

1900 Traveled in Italy before he returned to Finland

1900 October Received Diplome Commémoratif, Bronze, Silver, and Gold Medal for his work on the Finnish Pavilion for the Paris Exposition; Anatole France made favorable comment concerning Sarrinen's work on this building in an article for *Le Temps*

1902 Hvitträsk, a studio-home, was built by the firm members

1902 Met Jean Coquelin, French actor, during Coquelin's stay in Helsingfors

1903 Was offered position as professor in Kunstgewerbe-Schule in Düsseldorf, Germany; did not accept

1904 Was offered a professorship in Technische Hochschule, Berlin; did not accept

1904 March 6 Married Louise (Loja) Gesellius, sculptor, in Helsingfors

1904 Traveled with his wife, studying railroad stations in Germany, England, and Scotland

1905 Professor Lindgren, who became head of the architecture school in Helsingfors, withdrew from the firm; Gesellius and Saarinen continued as partners until 1907

1905 Visited Maxim Gorki in his Finnish country home at Kuokkala

1905 March 31 Eva-Lisa (Pipsan), a daughter, was born

1906 March Elected to membership in the Imperial Academy of Art in St. Petersburg, Russia; Count Louis Sparre and his brother-in-law, General Gustaf Mannerheim, conveyed this honor to Saarinen

1907 Gustav Mahler, composer and conductor of the Imperial Opera in Vienna, visited in the Saarinen home at the time of his giving a concert in Helsingfors; during his stay, Axel Gallén-Kallela painted Mahler's portrait

1907 Spring and summer Traveled with his wife through France, Switzerland, Austria, and Germany after taking his competition scheme for the Palace of Peace to The Hague; in Germany they met Professor Josef Olbrich at Darmstadt and Professor Peter Behrens at Düsseldorf

1907   Professor Géza Maróti, the sculptor, of Buda-pest, visited the Saarinens for the first time at Hvitträsk; he became a close friend of the family

1907   Autumn   Exhibited furniture in Salon d'Au-tomne in Paris

1907   Dissolution of the partnership of Gesellius and Saarinen

1908   Was invited to and took part in International Building Convention in Vienna, Austria

1909   July   One hundred and fifty Scandinavian ar-chitects met at a convention in Finland; the Saarinens gave a dinner for them at their home at Hvitträsk

1909   Was invited and took part in Die grosse Kunst-Ausstellung, an international art exhibition, in Berlin, Germany

1910   August 20   Eero, a son, was born.

1910   Traveled to Copenhagen and visited Martin Nyrop, the noted architect of the Copenhagen City Hall

1910   Traveled on the Continent with Julius Tallberg and Leo Lerche while doing research in city-planning

1910   Julius Meier-Graefe, German writer and art critic, was a house guest for an extended visit; at Hvitträsk he worked on his book on Cézanne

1910   August   Ugo Ojetti, of Florence, Italy, visited Hvitträsk; he was the art critic for Corriera della Sera in Milan

1910   Maxim Gorki visited Saarinen in his country home; from there he escaped Russian police and fled to Capri

1910–15   Worked on an extensive city-planning proj-ect of Munksnäs-Haga and published a book on the subject in 1915

1911   January   Was called as consultant in city-plan-ning by Reval, Estonia

1911   Was called to Budapest, Hungary, as expert in the town-planning of that city

1911   October   With his wife again met Gustav Mah-ler in Vienna

1911   October   Met Professor Josef Hoffman, archi-tect, in Vienna

1911–14   Being a member of the Imperial Academy of Art and the Modern Art Association, he visited often in St. Petersburg; he met there, among others, Diaghilev, Grabar, Leonid Andreyev, and Roerich

1912   Wrote a brochure on planning problems of Budapest, Hungary

1912   Traveled with his wife in Sweden, Denmark, and Germany

1912   Went with his wife to the Stockholm Olympiad, where he met, for the first time, Carl Milles and his wife Olga

1913   Published a brochure on a plan for the develop-ment of greater Reval, Estonia

1913   Was made corresponding member of Deutsche Werkbund in Germany and was invited to par-ticipate in the exhibition in Cologne in 1914

1913   October   Received Gold Medal for his exhibits in International Baufach Ausstellung at Leipzig

1913   Was made corresponding member of Die Zen-trale Vereinigung der Architekten Österreichs

1913   Traveled with his wife in Germany, Austria, and Italy; in Italy they visited Maxim Gorki at Capri

1914   Saarinen exhibited at Deutsche Werkbund Aus-stellung in Cologne, Germany

1914   The Italian government asked Saarinen to design the Axel Gallén-Kallela exhibition in the Inter-national Exhibition of Art in Venice

1915   October   Opening of the exhibition of the Munksnäs-Haga project at Riddarhuset in Hel-singfors

1916   Named to jury for city-planning competition for Bergen, Norway

1916   August   Was asked to become jury member for judging plans for Parliament House at Canberra, Australia

1917   After Saarinen's father fled from St. Petersburg early in the Bolshevik Revolution, he lived at Hvitträsk, where he later wrote his memoirs

1917–18   Worked on the city plan of greater Helsing-fors

1918   Honored by the government of Finland for his Railroad Station in Helsingfors. He was given the title of "Professor"

1919   Commissioned by the new Finnish government to work on designs for paper currency

1920   Became a member of the Finnish Academy of Art

1921   Father, Juho, died at Hvitträsk

1921   Was made a corresponding member of Iparmu-veszeti Tarsulat ("Society of Arts and Crafts"), Budapest

1922   May   Was made a corresponding member of the Freie Deutsche Academie des Städtebaues in Germany

1922   Went with his wife and daughter to Paris

1922   Entered international competition for the Tri-bune Tower in Chicago; won second prize

1923   Was elected vice-president of the International Federation for Town and Country Planning and Garden Cities; during the 1925 convention of this organization he met Raymond Unwin, En-glish city-planner, in New York

1923   February   Sailed for the United States on trip to visit with colleagues

1923   April   His family joined him; they lived in Evanston, Illinois, where he worked on his scheme for the development of the Chicago lake front

1924 Became visiting professor of architecture at the University of Michigan, which sponsored a large exhibition of his work at Ann Arbor

1924 Eric Mendelsohn, German architect, visited the Saarinens in Ann Arbor

1924 Became jury member of architectural competition for the Olympiad in Paris

1924 November Exhibited at the Thumb Tack Club's annual show at the Detroit Institute of Arts

1924 Became corresponding member of the Royal Institute of British Architects

1925 January Was made Commander, First Class, of the Finnish White Rose Order

1925 July Was made Honorary Doctor of Engineering of Technische Hochschule, the technical university of Karlsruhe, Germany

1925 Was asked by George G. Booth to develop the Cranbrook educational center at Bloomfield Hills, Michigan

1925 Daughter Pipsan married J. Robert F. Swanson, architect, of Bloomfield Hills

1925 He and his wife traveled to Paris Exposition

1925 Elected to honorary membership in the Michigan chapter of the American Institute of Architects

1925–39 The Saarinens made annual trips to Europe each summer, always stopping for a time in Finland

1926 January Exhibited in Ausstellung neuer amerikanischer Baukunst, an exhibition of newer American architecture, in Berlin

1926 Summer Took part in Scandinavian architects convention in Finland

1926 Was made honorary member of the Swedish Engineers Society of Detroit

1928 February Acted as judge and presented awards at the Indiana Society of Architects annual exhibition, Indianapolis, Indiana

1928 Summer Traveled back to Finland for an anniversary celebration of the erection of Hvitträsk; among the guests were Jean and Aino Sibelius and leading painters, sculptors, and architects of Finland

1929 Carl Milles visited Cranbrook, and, during his visit, Saarinen asked him to become resident sculptor and director of the department of sculpture at Cranbrook Academy of Art; he consented

1929 Elected as European representative to a jury for a competition for the Columbus Lighthouse Memorial, San Domingo; the two other members of the jury were Raymond Hood, representing the United States, and Horatio Acosta y Lara, representing South America; the judging of the first competition took place in Madrid, Spain

1930 Was made honorary member of the Architects' Society of Finland

1930 Traveled to Rio de Janeiro to judge the second competition for a Columbus Memorial Lighthouse, San Domingo; Frank Lloyd Wright, who replaced the late Raymond Hood on the jury, and Mrs. Wright accompanied him

1930 April Exhibited at the International Architectural and Arts Exposition, New York

1931 Joint exhibition of Loja and Eliel Saarinen was held at the gallery of the Architectural League of New York

1931 Became honorary member of the Architects' Society of Uruguay

1931 Became honorary member of the Central Institute of Architects of Brazil

1932 Exhibited in Nordiska Byggnadsdag, an architectural exhibition, Helsinki

1932 March Elected to membership in the Council of Confidence, the Art Academy of Finland

1932 June Appointed President of Cranbrook Academy of Art

1932 Received the degree of Honorary Doctor of Philosophy from the University of Helsinki

1932 Exhibition of arts and crafts by the entire Saarinen family in the Detroit Institute of Arts

1932 Was appointed jury member for architectural competition at the Olympiad, Los Angeles

1932 Summer Traveled with his son and daughter to Los Angeles for the judging

1933 Received the degree of Honorary Doctor of Architecture from the University of Michigan, Ann Arbor

1933 Received the Gold Medal of the Architectural League of New York at the annual exposition of the league in Grand Central Palace for his work on Cranbrook School for Boys

1934 Elected to honorary membership in Tekniska Högskolan i Helsingfors Student Förening, a student association in the Technical University of Helsinki

1934 Became a member of the Royal Academy of Art in Stockholm, Sweden

1934 Honorary member of the Society of Architects of Finland

1934 Received the degree of Honorary Doctor of Architecture from the Technical University of Finland, Helsinki

1935 March Acted as a jury member in a national competition for small-home designs, sponsored by General Electric

1935 Lectured on architecture at the School of Fine Arts, Yale University, New Haven

1935 Exhibition of arts and crafts by the Saarinen family at the Cranbrook Pavilion (now known as St. Dunstan's Playhouse)

1935 Was elected chairman of City and Regional Planning Committee, American Institute of Architects

1936 Received the degree of Honorary Doctor of Philosophy from Bethany College, Lindsborg, Kansas

1936 Was made honorary member of the Michigan Society of Architects and of the Detroit chapter of the American Institute of Architects

1937 Designed silver, executed by the International Silver Company, which was exhibited at Paris Exposition

1937 Summer   Traveled with his wife to the Paris Exposition

1937 Joint exhibition of Loja and Eliel Saarinen at the Norfolk Museum of Art and Science, Norfolk, Virginia

1939 Son Eero married Lily Swann, sculptor, of New York

1939 Received the Honorary Medal of the Academic Architects' Society, Copenhagen, Denmark

1940 Became Honorary Doctor of Arts, Harvard University, Cambridge, Massachusetts

1941 Became Master Architect of Alpha Rho Chi, architectural fraternity, Ann Arbor, Michigan

1942 Exhibited in "America Builds," a traveling exhibition in this country and Europe, sponsored and assembled by the Museum of Modern Art, New York

1942–47 Conducted town design classes at Cranbrook Academy of Art for a group of forty Detroit architects, called "Architects Civic Design Group"

1943 March   Saarinen and wife had an exhibition at Berea College, Berea, Kentucky

1943 *The City* was published by the Reinhold Publishing Corporation, New York; first paperback edition, MIT Press, 1965

1944 Enlarged photographs of Crow Island School, Winnetka, Illinois, were included in an exhibition of the New Architecture of the United States, sent to Cairo, Egypt

1944 Elected to fellowship in the American Institute of Architects

1944 November   Lectured at the Albright Art Gallery, Buffalo, New York

1945 December   He and Loja became citizens of the United States

1946 Honored by Finland's President Paasikivi with the Grand Cross of the Finnish Lion Order

1946 April   Elected an academician of the National Academy of Design

1946 June 30   Retired as President of Cranbrook Academy of Art. Continued as Director of the Department of Architecture and Urban Design

1946 Summer   With his wife traveled to Finland; while there they went to Järvenpää to visit with Jean and Aino Sibelius

1947 April   Received Gold Medal from the American Institute of Architects

1947 Completed his manuscript "Search for Form"

1947 Dissolution of the firm of Saarinen, Swanson, and Saarinen; father and son continued to work together in the organization Saarinen, Saarinen, and Associates

1948 Received Honorary Doctor of Laws degree, Drake University, Des Moines, Iowa

1948 His book *Search for Form* was published by the Reinhold Publishing Corporation, New York

1950 February   The Royal Institute of British Architects announced that Saarinen had been selected to receive its Royal Gold Medal for Architecture

1950 July 1   Died at his Cranbrook home

1950 July 5   Memorial service at Christ Church Cranbrook

1950 July 21   Morning memorial service at the University of Helsinki attended by his wife Loja and son Eero. Eulogies were delivered by Premier Urko Kekkonen and architect Alvar Aalto. Later in the day his ashes were taken to Hvitträsk for burial

1950 September 21   Eero accepted for his father the Royal Institute of British Architects Gold Medal at a meeting arranged by American Institute of Architects, Detroit, the Rackham Building

1951 April 15–May 6   Eliel Saarinen Memorial Exhibition, Museum of Cranbrook Academy of Art, Bloomfield Hills

1953 May 17   Inscribed memorial column dedicated in his honor, St. Dunstan's Chapel, Christ Church Cranbrook

1955 June 1–11   Eliel Saarinen Memorial Exhibition, Taidehalli (Art Hall), Helsinki

1955 November 3   Cranbrook Founder's Medal awarded posthumously to Saarinen, accepted by his wife Loja at Cranbrook House. A resolution adopted by the Board of Trustees May 5 was read at the presentation

1966 A foundation supported by both governmental and private subsidies was established to restore and preserve Hvitträsk as a Finnish national historical monument

1971 Crow Island School, Winnetka, Illinois, received 25-year award from American Institute of Architects

1973 Finland issued stamp commemorating Saarinen's birth

1977 Christ Church Lutheran, Minneapolis, received 25-year award from American Institute of Architects

OBITUARIES

American Institute of Architects Journal 14 (September 1950): 112–15, 138–39.

Architectural Forum 93 (August 1950): 82–83.

Architectural Record 108 (August 1950): 12.

Architectural Review 108 (September 1950): 203.

L'Architecture d'Aujourd'hui 20 (September 1950): IX.

Interiors 109 (July 1950): 134.

Progressive Architecture 31 (August 1950): 9.

Royal Institute of British Architects Journal 57 (July–August 1950): 333, 406.

Royal Institute of Canadian Architects Journal 27 (August 1950): 283.

Werk 37 (September 1950): Sup. 129.

Forum 6 (February 1951): 34–46.

LOUISE (LOJA) GESELLIUS SAARINEN

1879   March 16 Loja Gesellius was born to Hermann Otto Gesellius and wife, née Struckman

1899   Graduated from the Art School of the Finnish Academy of Art, Helsingfors

1892   She studied sculpture at Academy Colarossi, Paris, under the master Injalbert

1903   Returned to Helsingfors; joined her brother, working at commissions for sculpture, interiors, and photography

1904   March 6 Married Eliel Saarinen in Helsingfors

1904–50   Collaborated with her husband in making models for architecture and city planning; in creating and supervising the weaving of textiles, tapestries, etc.

1914–15   Made the large model of Munksnäs-Haga project, Riddarhuset in Helsingfors

1918   Received Cross of Liberty from Finnish government after the Civil War in Finland

1923   Exhibition of batiks with Pipsan, Evanston, Illinois

1928   Rugs and textiles for Saarinen residence, Cranbrook

1928–42   Founded and headed the Textile Department, Cranbrook Academy of Art

1929   Textiles for Richard Hudnut Salon, New York City

1929   Designed and supervised a team of weavers to execute the rugs, tapestries and textiles for Kingswood School, Cranbrook

1930   Rugs and textiles for Carl Milles residence, Cranbrook

1931   One-man exhibition of weaving and textiles, the Architectural League of New York

1932   One-man exhibition of weaving and textiles, the Detroit Institute of Art

1934   Exhibition at the Metropolitan Museum of Art

1935   Showed special weaving and textile collection with Pipsan, the Metropolitan Museum of Art

1935   Exhibition of weaving and textiles, with Pipsan and Robert Swanson, Museum of the Cranbrook Academy of Art

1937   Exhibited rugs and carpets, World Exposition, Paris

1937   Traveling exhibition for American Federation of Arts

1937   Silver Medal, International Exposition, Paris

1937   One-man exhibition, Norfolk Museum of Art and Science.

1938   Exhibition of weaving, Northwestern University, Evanston, Illinois

1938   Exhibition of weaving, Baltimore Museum of Art

1938   One-man exhibition at Cincinnati Museum of Art

1938   One-man exhibition at Toledo Museum of Art

1939   Exhibition of weaving at Golden Gate International Exhibition with Pipsan, San Francisco

1939–50   Innumerable commissions for architects and interior designers in various parts of the country

1940   Exhibited in Contemporary American Industrial Art Exhibition, Metropolitan Museum of Art

1940   Exhibited at Society of Arts and Crafts, Boston

1940   Exhibited at Philadelphia Art Alliance Galleries

1940   Included in Exhibition of Modern Textiles, University of Michigan Museum, Ann Arbor

1941   Exhibited at Museum of Modern Art, New York

1942   Exhibited at Toledo Museum of Art

1943   Exhibited at Baltimore Museum of Art

1943   Designed and wove tapestry for Tabernacle Church of Christ, Columbus, Indiana

1945   Exhibited at Dallas Museum of Fine Arts

1968   April 21 Died at Bloomfield Hills, Michigan

1968   Summer Loja's ashes returned to Finland by daughter Pipsan for burial at Hvitträsk

In every instance the first date given in the catalogue is the year in which Saarinen worked on the design. This date is also the one which accompanies illustrations throughout the text. Other dates in the catalogue entries refer to beginning and completion of executed plans.

FIRM OF GESELLIUS, LINDGREN, AND SAARINEN, HELSINGFORS

1897   Tallberg Apartment Building, Helsingfors. First and second prizes in competition.

1897   Market Building, Tammerfors, Finland. First prize in competition.

1898   Project: Verdandis Life Insurance Building, Åbo, Finland. Second prize in competition.

1898   Henry van Gilse van der Pals country estate, Paloniemi, Lojo, Finland.

1898   Project: Public Library, Åbo, Finland. First prize in competition.

1899   Finnish Pavilion at Paris Exposition, 1900. (Pl. 8.)
        Started 1899.   Completed 1900.
        Published in:
        Dekorative Kunst 3 (1900): 457–63.
        L'Architecture à l'Exposition Universelle de 1900, p. 65, Pl. X. Paris: Libraries-Imprimeries Réunies, 1900.

1899   Strömberg factory building, Helsingfors.

1899   Wuorio villa, Hästnäsund, Finland.

1899   Pohjola, a fire insurance building, Helsingfors.
        Published in:
        Innen-Dekoration 14 (December 1903): 289–306.
        Strengell, Gustaf, "Eliel Saarinen—Skyskrapans Nydanare."

1899   Wahl house, Viborg, Finland.

1899   Pellervo, a fire insurance building, Viborg, Finland.

1899   Heikel house, Helsingfors.

1900   Fabiansgatan 17, an apartment house, Helsingfors.

Published in:
Deutsche Kunst und Dekoration 13 (October 1903): 17–21.
Innen-Dekoration 14 (December 1903): 289–306.
Moderne Bauformen 3 (1904): 81–82.

1900   Dr. Törngren estate, Esbo, Finland.

1901   Dr. Sievers villa, Degerö, Finland.

1901   Olofsborg, an apartment house, Skatudden, Helsingfors.
        Published in:
        Innen-Dekoration 14 (December 1903): 289–306.

1901   Lutheran church, Janakkala, Finland.

1901   Grönmark villa, Lahti, Finland.

1901   Karsten villa, Helsingfors.

1901   Eol, an apartment house, Skatudden, Helsingfors.

1901   Sparbanken, a savings bank, Tammerfors, Finland.

1902   Hvitträsk, a studio-home for the members of the firm, near Helsingfors. Later became the private residence of Eliel Saarinen. (Pls. 9–18.)
        Started 1902.
        Published in:
        Moderne Bauformen 6, no. 4 (1907): 159–62; 8, no. 8 (1909): 350, 353.
        Hemma och Ute 3 (August 1913): 210–14; 3 (September 1913): 234–35.
        American Architect and Architectural Review 124 (September 26, 1923): 19 pls.
        Arkkitehti nos. 11–12 (1943): 24.
        Architectural Review 139 (February 1966): 152–54.
        Space Design no. 133 (September 1975): 91–94.
        Connaissance des Arts no. 238 (December 1971): 108–13, 192.
        New York Times 13 February 1966, VI, p. 64

1902   Westerlund estate, Hvittorp (near Helsingfors), Finland
        Published in:
        Moderne Bauformen 4, no. 2 (1905), pls. 80, 82.

1902. HELSINGFORS. NATIONAL MUSEUM

1902 National Museum, Helsingfors. First prize in competition.
Started 1902. Completed 1904.
Published in:
Moderne Bauformen 6, no. 4 (1907): 145–50.

1902 Suur-Merijoki, a country estate, Viborg, Finland. (Pls. 19–23.)
Published in:
Moderne Bauformen 4, no. 3 (1905): 45–48, pls. 25–32, 40–42.

1902 Direktor Rudolf Elving country estate, Kirjokivi.

1902 Woikka Bruk, a paper mill, Kymmene, Finland.

1902 Pirtti, an art club, Helsingfors.

1902 Miekkakala, an apartment building, Helsingfors.

1902 Lutheran church parish house, Jokkis, Finland.

1902 Public Library, Uleåborg, Finland. First prize in competition.

1902 Albert Edelfelt villa, Haikko, Finland.

1902 Selin villa, Sökö, Finland.

1903 Project: Lutheran church, Nilsiä, Finland.
Published in:
Moderne Bauformen 4, no. 2 (1905): 24, pls. 15, 16.

1903 Project: Bobrinsky villa, Moscow. Plans included a design for the complete interior.
Published in:
Moderne Bauformen 3 (1904): 80–84, pls. 81–86.

1904 Luther factory building, Reval, Estonia.

1904 Count Schouvaloff memorial, Kursk, Russia.

1904 Bank building, Sortavala, Finland.

1904 Methodist church, Helsingfors.

1904 Nordiska Föreningsbanken, a bank, Helsingfors.
Published in:
Moderne Bauformen 6, no. 4 (1907): 141–44.
Arkitekten 31, no. 4 (1934): 31.

1904 Haus eines Kunst Freundes, a private residence, Essen, Ruhr, Germany. Second prize in international competition.

Published in:
Moderne Bauformen 6, no. 4 (1907): 137–40.

1904 Railroad station, Helsingfors. First prize in competition. (Pls. 30–37.)
Started 1905. Completed 1914.
The structure was built in two parts; administration section, 1905–9; the station proper, 1910–14. In 1914 it was converted for use as a Russian military hospital. In 1919 it was opened as a railroad station.
7,000,000 Finnish marks. 240,000 cubic meters (7,200,000 cu. ft.).
Published in:
Moderne Bauformen 6, no. 4 (1907): 151–56.
Der Verkehr, p. 41. Jena: Eugen Diederichs, 1914.
Western Architect 31 (May 1922): Pls. I–V.
American Architect and Architectural Review, 124 (26 September 1923): 19 pls.
Suomen Kuvalehti 11 (December 1927): 2074–75; 12 (7 January 1928), cover.
Architectural Forum 53 (December 1930): 655–94.
Arkitekten 35, no. 2 (1938), p. 18.

1904 Railroad Station, Viborg, Finland. Both first and second prizes were won by the firm.
Published in:
Moderne Bauformen 6, no. 4 (1907): 157–58.
Architectural Forum 53 (December 1930): 655–94.

1904 Päivälehti, a newspaper building, Helsingfors.

FIRM OF GESELLIUS AND SAARINEN HELSINGFORS

1905 Dr. Paul Remer country estate, Molchow-Haus, Mark Brandenburg, Germany. (Pls. 24–29.)
Started 1905. Completed 1907.
Design included plans for the complete interior.
Published in:
Moderne Bauformen 7, no. 6 (1908): 217–39; 8, no. 8 (1909): pl. 55.
Dekorative Kunst 11 (June 1908): 377–92.

1905 Project: Palace of Peace, The Hague. Competition to which twenty-four architects were given special invitation.
Published in:
Veckans Krönika no. 35 (October 1906): 565–67.

1905 Arbetarföreningens hus, a workmen's labor-union building, Kotka, Finland.

1906 Helsingin Sanomat, a newspaper building, Helsingfors.

1906 Oma, an apartment building, Helsingfors.

1906 Project: Town Hall, Villmanstrand, Finland.
Published in:
Moderne Bauformen 8, no. 8 (1909): 341.

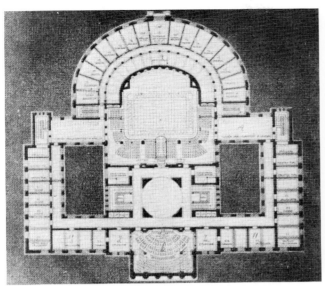

1908. HELSINGFORS. LANDTDAGSHUSET. HOUSE OF PARLIAMENT. MAIN FLOOR PLAN

DISSOLUTION OF THE PARTNERSHIP OF GESELLIUS AND SAARINEN

1907 Project: Public school, Helsingfors.
Published in:
Moderne Bauformen 8, no. 8 (1909): 343–44.

1907 Three rooms: living room, dining room, and library for Keirkner house, Skatudden, Helsingfors.
Published in:
Moderne Bauformen 8, no. 8 (1909): 351–52.

1908 Project: Landtdagshuset, House of Parliament, Helsingfors. First prize in competition. (Frontispiece, Pls. 56, 58.)

1908. HELSINGFORS. ART EXHIBITION HALL

1909. LADOGA, FINLAND. DR. WINTER VILLA

Published in:
Arkitektur och Dekorativ Konst 38 (April 1908): 41–44.
Teknisk-Tidskrift 38 (April 1908): 41–44.
Moderne Bauformen 8, no. 8 (1909): 345–47.
Bouwkunding Weekblad 34 (April 1914): 185–86.
Western Architect 31 (May 1922): Pl. V.
Builder 125 (August 1923): 209.

1908 Project: Art Exhibition Hall, Helsingfors.
Published in:
Moderne Bauformen 8, no. 8 (1909): 348.

1908 Project: Public school, Åbo, Finland.
Published in:
Moderne Bauformen 8, no. 8 (1909): pl. 56.

1908 Project: Salamandra Insurance Building, St. Petersburg, Russia.

1909 Dr. Winter villa, Ladoga, Finland.
Published in:
Cahiers d'art, January, 1926, p. 12.

1909 Rådhuset, City Hall, Joensuu, Finland. First prize in competition.
Started 1912. Completed 1913.
Published in:
American Architect and Architectural Review 124 (26 September 1923): 19 pls.

1909 Project: Cederberg mausoleum, Joensuu, Finland.
Published in:
Moderne Bauformen 8, no. 8 (1909): 342.

1910 Tammerfors Teater, a playhouse. Second prize in competition.

1910 Tallberg Passage, a group of office buildings centered around an arcade, Helsingfors. First prize in competition.

1910 Industriutställning, "Industrial Exposition Plan," Helsingfors. First prize in competition.

1909. JOENSUU, FINLAND. CEDERBERG MAUSO-
LEUM

1910   Hubers Affärspalats, an office building, Helsing-
       fors. First prize in competition.

1910–15 City-planning, Munksnäs-Haga, Finland.
       Model of the plan opened for exhibition at
       Riddarhuset, Helsingfors, October, 1915. (Pls.
       39–42.)
       Published in:
       Saarinen, Eliel. *Munksnäs-Haga.* With "Stads-
       planskonst" by Gustaf Strengell. Helsingfors:
       Lilius & Hertzberg, 1915. Pp. 123 with addi-
       tional photographs and diagrams.
       Arkitekten 6, no. 6 (1915): 73–77; 6, no. 7
       (1915): 89–92; 19 (January 1917): 129–32.
       Teknillinen Aikakauslehti no. 10 (October
       1915): 149–54.
       Nya Argus no. 22 (November 1915): 199–200.
       Veckans Krönika 11 (October 1915): 355–56.
       Hemma och Ute 5 (15 November 1915): 302–3.
       Otava no. 11 (November 1915): 505–12.
       Kommunaltidskrift 1 (January 1916): 14–15.
       Der Städtebau 22, nos. 3–4 (1920): 21–27, 7 pls.
       Pencil Points 22 (September 1936): 68–69.

1911   City Hall, Lahti, Finland. First prize in competi-
       tion.
       Started 1911.   Completed 1912.

1911   Estobank, a bank, Reval, Estonia. First prize in
       international competition.
       Started 1911.   Completed 1912.

1911–13 City-planning, Reval, Estonia. Received first
       prize in international competition for a city
       plan for Reval, April, 1913. (Pls. 45–48.)
       Published in:
       Der Städtebau 18, nos. 5/6 (1921): 45–56, pls.
       21–26.

1912   Project: City-plan for Canberra, Australia. Sec-
       ond prize in international competition. (Pls.
       49–52.)
       Published in:
       Arkitektur no. 12 (December 1912): 141–57.
       Der Städtebau 10, No. 7 (1913): 73–77, 86–88.

1912   Project: Suomi Life Insurance Building, Hel-
       singfors. Second prize in competition.

1912   Gewerbevereinshaus. Craft Association Build-
       ing, Riga, Latvia. First prize in international
       competition.

1912   Girls' school, Lahti, Finland.
       Started 1912.   Completed 1912.

1912   Project: Rådhuset, City Hall, Reval, Estonia.

1913   Johan Wilhelm Snellman monument, Helsing-
       fors. First prize in competition.
       Sculpture done for the monument was by Emil
       Wikström.

1913   Project: St. Paul's Lutheran Church, Dorpat,
       Estonia.
       Without Saarinen's knowledge, this design was
       badly executed during the war.
       Published in:
       Bouwkundig Weekblad 34 (April 1914): 198–
       202.

1914   Project: Finnish Lutheran congregation build-
       ing, St. Petersburg.
       Not executed because of the war.

1914   Project: Finnish Pavilion, San Francisco Exposi-
       tion. First prize in competition.
       Not executed because of the war.

1911. LAHTI, FINLAND. CITY HALL

1913. DORPAT, ESTONIA. ST. PAUL'S LUTHERAN CHURCH

1914 Design for the Axel Gallén-Kallela exhibition in the International Exhibition of Art, Venice. This design was requested by the city of Venice.

1915 Keirkner Art Gallery, Helsingfors.
Published in:
American Architect and Architectural Review 124 (26 September 1923): 19 pls.

1916 Project: House of Parliament, Canberra, Australia.
Competition later called off because of the war.
Published in:
Michigan Architect and Engineer 6 (January 1924), cover and Frontispiece.

1916 Centralgatan, Helsingfors. Designed and built, in part, this cut-through street in Helsingfors.

1916 Project: Redesigned Swedish Playhouse, Helsingfors.

1917 Nikolai Tirkkonen office building, Helsingfors. Not built because of the war.

1917 Nikolai Tikkonen house, Munksnäs-Haga, Finland.
Not built because of the war.

1917–18 City-plan, Greater Helsingfors. (Pls. 43–44.)
Published in:
Jung, Bertel. *Suur-Helsinki.* Helsinki: Lilius & Hertzberg, 1918. Pp. 18.
Bouwkundig Weekblad 40 (25 October 1919): 262–65.
Der Städtebau 7, nos. 3/4 (1920): 21–27, pls. 13–19.
Arkitekten 28 (1931): 150–53; 24, no. 11 (1932): 163–69; 30, no. 8 (1933): 111–12; 31, no. 4 (1934): 59–60; 34, no. 3 (1937): 33–39.
Pencil Points 17 (September 1936): 465–94.
Helsingin Kaiku 13 (19 November 1915): 379–84.

1919 Project: Hospital, Cairo, Egypt. International competition. (Pls. 67–69.)
Published in:
Pencil Points 17 (September 1936): 465–94.

1919 Project: Kalevalatalo, a Finnish museum, Munksnäs, Finland. (Pls. 61–66.)
Published in:
Arkkitehti nos. 11–12 (1943): 45–50.
Kalevalatalo. Helsinki: Kalevalaseura, Otava, 1921. Pp. 14+11 pls.

1920 Munksnäs Pensionat, a hotel, Munksnäs, Finland.

1922 Project: Tribune Tower, Chicago. (Pls. 59, 70–72.)
Associate architects: Dwight G. Wallace and Bertell Grenman.
Second prize in international competition sponsored by the *Chicago Tribune.*
Published in:
The International Competition for a New Administration Building for the Chicago Tribune, MCMXXII, pp. 57–59, pls. 13–19. Chicago: Tribune Co., 1923.
Architectural Record 53 (February 1923): 151–57.
Architecture 47 (January 1923): 14; 47 (March 1923): 87–88.
Architekten 25 (February 1923): 22–27 (published in Copenhagen).
Byggnads-Tidningen 14, no. 3 (1923): 33–39.
Wasmuths Monatshefte für Baukunst 8 (1924): 296–309.
Baukunst 2 (April 1926): 142–43.
Woltersdorf, Arthur. *Living Architecture,* pl. XII. Chicago: A. Kroch, 1930.
Pencil Points 17 (September 1936): 465–94.
Archi 23 (June 1942): 53–56.
Society of Architectural Historians Journal 6 (July–December 1947): 1–5.
Sky, Alison, and Stone, Michelle, *Unbuilt America.* New York: McGraw-Hill, 1976.
Preservation News 17 (May 1977): 9.

1923 Project: Chicago lake front plan. (Pls. 73–78.)
Published in:
American Architect and Architectural Review
124 (5 December 1923): 487–514.
Arkitekten 4, no. 2 (1924): 15–28.
Architectural Forum 116 (May 1962): 214.

1924 Project: Detroit river front development. This
plan included drawings for a Memorial Hall.
Published in:
*Memorial Hall: A Report Made by Detroit City
Council.* June, 1924.
*Fourth Annual Exhibition of the Thumb Tack
Club.* Detroit, 1924.
American Architect 124 (20 April 1926): 481–
82.
Architectural Forum 55 (October 1931): 271.

1925 Project: The President Burton Memorial, University of Michigan, Ann Arbor.
Memorial designed at request of the student
body.

1925 Project: A Christian Science church, Minneapolis, Minnesota.

Published in:
Pencil Points 17 (September 1936): 486.

1925 Cranbrook School for Boys, Bloomfield Hills,
Michigan. Rebuilt from farmhouse group.
(Pls. 79–85.)
Started 1926. Completed 1930.
$3,212,000. 3,908,000 cubic feet.
Published in:
Architectural Record 64 (December 1928): 452–
60, 475–506, 525–28, frontispiece.
Architectural Progress 5 (August 1931).
Country Life 68 (June 1935): 10–15.
Michigan Engineer 59 (Convention no., 1940):
2, photographs on cover, and 4.

1926–41 Cranbrook Academy of Art, Bloomfield
Hills, Michigan. (Pls. 103–5.)
$1,361,000. 1,420,000 cubic feet.
Published in:
Architectural Record 68 (December 1930): 444–
51.
London Studio 24 (Studio 124) (November
1942): 159–61.
Harper's Bazaar 72 (1 March 1939): 89–90, 119–
20.
Octagon 6 (July 1934): 11.
Magazine of Art 22 (February 1931): 142–43.
Space Design no. 134 (October 1934): 99–105.
Archi 23 (June 1942): 59.
L'Architecture d'Aujourd'hui 20, Sup. 7 (April
1950): 57–58.
Progressive Architecture 58 (August 1977): 53.
The New Republic 178 (24 June 1978): 27–30.

1925. ANN ARBOR, MICHIGAN. THE UNIVERSITY
OF MICHIGAN. THE PRESIDENT BURTON ME-
MORIAL

1925. MINNEAPOLIS, MINNESOTA. A CHRISTIAN
SCIENCE CHURCH. AUDITORIUM

1927 Project: Palace of League of Nations, Geneva. International competition.
Published in:
Architectural Record 63 (May 1928): 398–99.
Sixth Annual Exhibition of the Thumb Tack Club. Detroit, 1928.

1928 Eliel Saarinen residence, Cranbrook Academy of Art, Bloomfield Hills, Michigan. (Pls. 151–56.)
Started 1928. Completed 1929.
Rugs and draperies designed by Loja Saarinen.
Published in:
Architectural Record 68 (December 1930): 448, 450–51.
Suomen Kuvalehti 15 (19 September 1931): cover and 1532–33.
Master Builder 39 (August 1934): 231–36.
House Beautiful 74 (October 1933): 133–36.
Pencil Points 17 (September 1936): 479–80.
Progressive Architecture 55 (July 1974): 70–75.

1929 Project: Chicago War Memorial, Chicago, Illinois.

1929 Kingswood School for Girls, Cranbrook, Bloomfield Hills, Michigan. (Pls. 86–97.)
Started 1929. Completed 1930.
$1,786,000. 2,109,000 cubic feet.
Published in:
Architectural Forum 56 (January 1932): 37–60.
Suomen Kuvalehti 16 (7 May 1932): 692–93.
Arkitekten 29 (1932): 33–43.
Country Life 73 (June 1935): 10–15.
Pencil Points 17 (September 1936): 484–85; 18 (October 1937): 651–58.

1929 Dining room, designed for "The Architect and Industrial Art," an exhibition at the Metropolitan Museum, New York.
Published in:
Architectural Forum 61 (December 1934): 412–13.

1929 Hudnut Building, New York.
Ely Jacques Kahn, associate.
Started 1929. Completed 1930.
Saarinen designed both exterior and interior.
Rugs designed and woven by Loja Saarinen.
Published in:
Architectural Forum 55 (October 1931): 415–22.

1931 The Institute of Science, Cranbrook, Bloomfield Hills, Michigan. (Pls. 98–102.)
Started 1931. Completed 1933.
$238,000. 538,000 cubic feet.
Published in:
Museum News 14 (15 June 1936): 14.
Architectural Forum 69 (December 1938): 418–24.

1931 Project: Comprehensive scheme of buildings, Stevens Institute of Technology, Hoboken, New Jersey.

1932 Project: Design for the Chrysler site at the Century of Progress Exposition, Chicago, 1933. Participated with a selected group of architects in competition.

1927. GENEVA. PALACE OF LEAGUE OF NATIONS

1933 Project: Alexander Hamilton Memorial, commissioned by Miss Kate Buckingham, Chicago, Illinois.

1933. CHICAGO. ALEXANDER HAMILTON MEMORIAL. MODEL

1934 Room for a lady, designed for "The Architect and Industrial Art," an exhibition at the Metropolitan Museum, New York.
Loja and Eliel Saarinen, designers.
Published in:
Architectural Forum 61 (December 1934): 312–13.

1935 Project: Alkohooliliike Building, Helsinki.

1937 Community House, Fenton, Michigan.
Assisted by son, Eero Saarinen.
Started 1937. Completed 1938.
$80,000 (approximately). 160,000 cubic feet.
Published in:
Pencil Points 23 (November 1942): 46–60.

1938 General scheme and music shed (symphony pavilion), Berkshire Music Center, Tanglewood, Stockbridge, Massachusetts. (Pls. 141–43.)
Started 1938. Completed 1938.
Published in:
Architectural Record 85 (January 1939): 44–45.
Life 11 (1 September 1941): 74–75.

1938 Kleinhans Music Hall, Buffalo, New York. (Pls. 106–16.)
Eliel and Eero Saarinen, designers; F. J. and W. A. Kidd, architects.

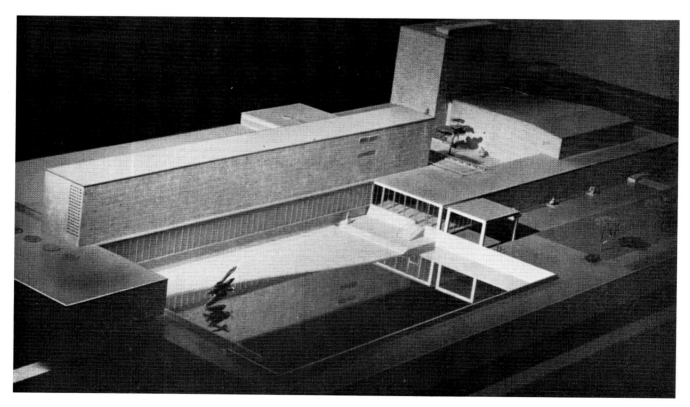

1939. WASHINGTON, D.C. SMITHSONIAN ART GALLERY. MODEL. AERIAL VIEW. ". . . a continuous window strip which overlooks a court and the promenade on the borders of the pool . . ." *Photo by Askew*

1940. CRANBROOK ACADEMY OF ART. MUSEUM AND LIBRARY. ARCADE. ". . . a motif that is highly personal but at the same time universal . . ." *Photo by Hedrich-Blessing*

Started 1938.   Completed 1940.
$1,500,000 (approximately).   2,760,000 cubic feet (approximately).
Published in:
Architectural Record 89 (February 1941): 88.
Architectural Forum 75 (July 1941), 35–42.
Kleinhans Music Hall. Buffalo: Kleinhans Music Hall Management, 1942.
L'Architecture d'Aujourd'hui 20 (May 1949): 16

1938   Project: Campus plan, Goucher College, Baltimore, Maryland. Second prize in competition. Eliel and Eero Saarinen, architects.

1939   Crow Island School, Winnetka, Illinois. (Pls. 131–36.)
Eliel and Eero Saarinen, Perkins, Wheeler and Will, architects.
Started 1939.   Completed 1940.
Published in:
Architectural Forum 75 (August 1941): 79–92.
Architectural Record 91 (January 1942): 3–4.
The American School and University, pp. 37–42. New York: American School Pub., 1943.
Built in U.S.A. 1932–1944. With Foreword by Philip L. Goodwin. Edited by Elizabeth Mock. New York: Museum of Modern Art, 1944.

1939   Project: Smithsonian Art Gallery, Washington, D.C. First prize in competition. (Pls. 137–40.)
Eliel and Eero Saarinen, architects; J. Robert F. Swanson, associate.
Published in:
Architectural Forum 72 (July 1939): i–xvi.
Architectural Record 86 (August 1939): 50.
Magazine of Art 32 (August 1939): 456–59, 488–89.
Museum News 17 (1 September 1939): 1.
Pencil Points 22 (August 1941): 497–516.
Built in U.S.A. 1932–1944. With Foreword by Philip L. Goodwin. Edited by Elizabeth Mock. New York: Museum of Modern Art, 1944.

1940   Museum and Library, Cranbrook Academy of Art, Bloomfield Hills, Michigan. (Pls. 144–50.)
Started 1942.   Completed 1943.
$476,000.   726,000 cubic feet.
Published in:
Museum News 18 (1 September 1940): 1.
Art Digest 17 (January 1943): 13.
Magazine of Art 36 (January 1943): 6–9.
Pencil Points 24 (December 1943): 36–49.

1941. CENTER LINE, MICHIGAN. CENTER LINE HOUSING SCHEME. MODEL

1940 Tabernacle Church of Christ (now First Christian Church), Columbus, Indiana. (Pls. 60, 117–26.)
Eliel and Eero Saarinen, architects.
Started 1941. Completed 1942.
$750,000. 1,675,000 cubic feet.
Published in:
Time 37 (27 January 1941): 39–40.
Architectural Forum 77 (October 1942): 35–44; 123 (December 1965) 40–49.
Architectural Record 93 (March 1943): 69–84.
Shane Quarterly 4 (October 1943): 244–46, 247–57.
Inland Architect 16, no. 10 (December 1972): 9–13.

1941 Project: large auditorium, small theater, and inn, Oberlin College, Oberlin, Ohio.
Eliel and Eero Saarinen, architects; Richard Kimball, associate architect.

1941 500-dwelling-unit defense housing, school and community house, Center Line, Michigan.
Saarinen, Swanson, and Saarinen, architects.
Started 1941. Completed 1941.
Published in:
Architectural Forum 75 (October 1941): 220–31; 76 (May 1942): 281–84.
Pencil Points 23 (November 1942): 46–60.

1941 A. C. Wermuth house, Fort Wayne, Indiana. (Pls. 127–30.)
Eliel and Eero Saarinen, architects.
Started 1941. Completed 1942.

1941 Willow Run housing units, Michigan.
Saarinen, Swanson, and Saarinen, architects.
Started 1941. Completed 1942.
Published in:
Architectural Record 92 (July 1942): 47; 94 (October 1943): 54–60.

1942 Town Center, Willow Run, Michigan.
Saarinen, Swanson, and Saarinen, architects.
Started 1942. Completed 1942.
Published in:
Architectural Forum 78 (March 1943): 38–41.

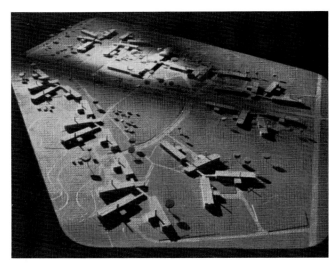

1941. WILLOW RUN HOUSING UNITS, MICHIGAN. MODEL. *Photo by Munroe*

1943. WASHINGTON, D.C. LINCOLN HEIGHTS HOUSING CENTER

1944. NEW CASTLE, INDIANA. TOWN CENTER.
Photo by Harvey Croze

1942   Schools, Willow Run, Michigan.
Saarinen, Swanson, and Saarinen, architects.
Started 1942. Completed 1942.

1942   Project: Group-plan and architectural scheme, Wayne University, Detroit, Michigan. Second prize in competition.
Saarinen, Swanson, and Saarinen, architects.

1943   Lincoln Heights housing center, Washington, D.C.
Saarinen, Swanson, and Saarinen, architects.

1943–44   Project: Parliament Building, Quito, Ecuador.
Submitted in international competition.

1944   Summer opera house and chamber music hall, Berkshire Music Center, Tanglewood, Stockbridge, Massachusetts. (Pl. 143.)
Eliel and Eero Saarinen, architects.
Started 1944. Completed 1944.
Published in:
Progressive Architecture (Pencil Points) 28 (March 1947): 53–58.
Architectural Review 101 (May 1947): 163–64.
L'Architecture d'Aujourd'hui 20 (May 1949): 19–21.

SAARINEN, SWANSON, AND SAARINEN

1944   Town planning, New Castle, Indiana.

1944   The Edmundson Memorial Museum, Des Moines Art Center, Des Moines, Iowa. (Pls. 165–73.)
Brooks-Borg, associate architects.
Started 1946. Completed 1948.
$800,000.
Published in:
Art Digest 21 (October 1946): 19
Art Digest 22 (May 1948): 15
Art Digest 22 (July 1948): 9–10

Museum News 26 (15 June 1948): 1
Architectural Forum 91 (July 1949): 65–69.
L'Architecture d'Aujourd'hui 20, Sup. 6 (April 1950): 55–56.

1945   Women's dormitory building, Antioch College, Yellow Springs, Ohio. (Pl. 183.)
Max G. Mercer, associate architect.
Started 1946. Completed 1949.
$450,000.
Published in:
Progressive Architecture 30 (July 1949): 56; 30 (August 1949): 49–53, 89.

1945   General Motors Technical Center, Detroit, Michigan. (Pls. 174–79.)
$20,000,000.
Published in:
Architectural Forum 82 (August 1945): 7; 91 (July 1949): 70–78; 95 (November 1951): 111–23; 98 (February 1953): 145; 134 (June 1971): 22–28.
Architectural Record 98 (September 1945): 16; 98 (November 1945): 98–103; 110 (October 1951): 12.
Pencil Points 26 (September 1945): 16.
Architect and Engineer 163 (October 1945): 12.
Interiors 111 (November 1951): 12.
The Architect's Yearbook 5 (1953): 133–69.

1944. TANGLEWOOD, STOCKBRIDGE, MASSACHUSETTS. BERKSHIRE MUSIC CENTER. OPERA HOUSE. FRONT VIEW. *Photo by Gottscho-Schleisner*

1945. DETROIT, MICHIGAN. GENERAL MOTORS TECHNICAL CENTER. FRONT VIEW. STYLING BUILD-ING. *Rendering by Eero Saarinen*

Architect and Building News 210 (September 1956): 418–21.
Werk 44 (February 1957): 58–64.

1945 Planning, Washtenaw County, Michigan.

1945 Campus development plan, Antioch College, Yellow Springs, Ohio. (Pls. 180–83.)
Max G. Mercer, associate architect.
Published in:
Architectural Record 102 (December 1947): 71–87.

1945 Project: Fort Wayne Art School and Museum, Fort Wayne, Indiana. $600,000.

1946 Campus development plan, Drake University, Des Moines, Iowa. (Pl. 192.)
Published in:
Architectural Record 102 (December 1947): 71–87.

1946 Project: Metropolitan Milwaukee War Memorial, Milwaukee, Wisconsin.
$5,000,000.
Published in:
Architectural Record 102 (November 1947): 74–77.

SAARINEN, SAARINEN, AND ASSOCIATES

1946 Project: Community development plan for the estate of H. H. Houston, deceased. Outer Roxborough, Philadelphia, Pennsylvania.

1946 Project: Christ Church, Cincinnati, Ohio.
$1,000,000.
Published in:
Architectural Forum 91 (December 1949): 60.

1947 Detroit civic center, Detroit, Michigan. Design only.
Published in:
Interiors 108 (July 1949): 18.
Architectural Forum 90 (April 1949): 12–13.

1947 Campus development plan, Stephens College, Columbia, Missouri.

1947 Project: Chapel, Stephens College, Columbia, Missouri.
$375,000
Published in:
Progressive Architecture 32 (June 1951): 15–16.

1947 Project: Peoples Bank and Trust Company, Fort Wayne, Indiana.
$800,000.

1947 Christ Church Lutheran, Minneapolis, Minnesota.
$300,000.
Hills, Gilbertson, and Hayes, associates.
Started 1948. Completed 1949.
Published in:
Architectural Forum 93 (July 1950): 80–85.
L'Architecture d'Aujourd'hui 21 (December 1950–January 1951): 79–83.
Albert Christ-Janer and Mary Mix Foley, *Modern Church Architecture*. New York: McGraw-Hill, 1962
American Institute of Architects Journal 66 (May 1977): 28–29.

GENERAL BIBLIOGRAPHY

Adams, Robert W. "Shall Detroit Have a New Civic Center?" *Detroiter* 15 (7 July 1924): 5–8.

Ahrenberg, J. "Fredspalatset i Haag." *Veckans Krönika,* no. 35 (October 1906) pp. 565–67.

———. "Gesellius, Lindgren, und Saarinen." *Moderne Bauformen* 3 (1904): 80–84, pls. 81–86.

———. "Das Landgut 'Merijoki'" *Moderne Bauformen* 4 (1905): 45–48, color pls. 25–36, 40–42.

——— "Der neue Stil in Finnland." *Moderne Bauformen* 3 (1904): 81–86 and 5 color pls.

Akademie der Künste zu Berlin. *Ausstellung neuer amerikanischer Baukunst.* Berlin, 1926. Pp. 83+xv pls.

American Architects from the First World War to the Present. Vol. 4 in the Art and Architecture Information Guide Series. Edited by Lawrence Wodehouse. Detroit: Gale Research, 1977. xii+305 p.

"Americans at Cranbrook." *Art Digest* 14 (15 April 1940): 7.

Aminoff, Berndt. "Helsingin Asemakaavakysymyksiä." *Helsingin Kaupungin Keskiosien Yleisasemakaavaehdotus* (Helsinki, 1932), pp. 6–50.

———. "Två Huvudstäder." *Arkitekten* 28 (11), no. 10 (1931): 150–53.

Andersin, Harald. "Generalplanen." *Arkitekten* 30, no. 12 (1933): 75–77.

"An Announcement of the Third Post-graduate Program at Cranbrook, Architectural Department." *Architectural Record* 73 (June, 1933): 431–32.

"Antioch College Dormitory for Women." *Progressive Architecture* 30 (June 1949): 56; 30 (August 1949): 49–53, 89.

"Architectural Overtones: Photographs of Work of Carl Milles on the Grounds in Cranbrook." *American Architect and Architecture* 150 (January 1937): 39–46.

L'Architecture á l'Exposition universelle de 1900. Paris: Libraries-Imprimeries Réunies, 1900. Pp. 100.

"Art Center in Des Moines, Iowa." *Architectural Forum* 91 (July 1949): 65–69.

"Art of Weaving: Cranbrook Looms," *Design* 38 (December 1936): 28–29.

Asada, Takashi. "The Studio Home by Lake Hvitträsk, in the Western Suburbs of Helsinki." *Space Design* no. 133 (September 1975): 91–94.

Avenard, Étienne. "L'Exposition finlandaise au Salon d'Automne." *Art et decoration,* November 1908, pp. 137–46.

"Automobile Research Center: General Motors Technical Center 20 Years after First Phase Completion, Detroit, Michigan." *Architectural Forum* 134 (June 1971): 22–28.

Badovici, Jean. "La Maison d'aujourd'hui." *Cahiers d'art,* January 1926, p. 12.

Bailey, Anson. "The Home of Eliel Saarinen at the Cranbrook Academy of Art." *Master Builder* 39 (August 1934): 231–36.

"Der Bahnhof." *Der Verkehr: Jahrbuch des Deutschen Werkbundes.* Jena: Eugene Diederichs, 1914. P. 41.

Banderillero. "Munksnäs-Haga utställningen i Riddarhuset." *Veckans Krönika* 11 (October 1915): 355–56.

Barker, Kent. "Eliel Saarinen . . . an Appreciation." *Journal of the Royal Architectural Institute of Canada* 21 (December 1944): 269–84.

"Barndomsminnenas värld." *Vårbrodd,* 1929, pp. 54–86.

Behrendt, Walter Curt. *Modern Building.* New York: Harcourt, Brace & Co., 1937. Pp. 241+pls.

"Die beiden ersten Preise des Chicagoer Tribune Tower-Wettbewerbes." *Baukunst* 2 (April 1926): 142–43.

Beutinger, E. "Die moderne Kunst-Bewegung in Finnland." *Deutsche Kunst und Dekoration* 13 (October 1903): 17–21.

Birck, F. W. "Finnische Architekten." *Lübecksche Blätter* 63 (September 1921): 349–50.

Blomstedt, Aulis. "Eliel Saarinen." *Arkkitehti* nos. 11–12 (1943): 145. This article, with a portrait of Saarinen included, is the first in a series of this issue of *Arkkitehti* partially dedicated to Saarinen on the anniversary of his seventieth birthday.

Blomstedt, P. E. "Helsingfors Framtid." *Arkitekten,* 29 no. 11 (1932): 163–69.

———. "Stadsplaneproblem i Centrum av Stor-Helsingfors." *Arkitekten* 33, no. 3 (1937): 33–39.

Bokland, Harald. "Arkitektutflykten till Finland," *Byggnadstidningen* no. 14 (July 1909): 170–71.

Brock, H. I. "In Defense of City-Planners." *New York Times,* July 9, 1944.

———. "In Defense of City Planners." *Weekly Bulletin, Michigan Society of Architects* 17 (25 July 1944): 1, 4.

Byggnadskonst i Finland. Handbook sponsored by Finlands Arkitektforbund. Helsingfors, 1932. Pp. 200.

Cain, Theron I., "The City." *Journal of Aesthetics* 3, no. 11 (1945): 87.

"A Campus Plan under Way. I. Drake University; II. Antioch College." *Architectural Record* 102 (December, 1947): 71–87.

"Center Line: 476 Permanent Units." *Architectural Forum* 76 (May 1942): 281–84.

"Center Line Defense Houses." *Architectural Forum* 75 (October 1941): 229–31.

"Center Line School-Community Center." *Pencil Points* 23 (November 1942): 56–60.

"Centre des Arts, Cité Des Moines." *L'Architecture d'Aujourd'hui* 20 (April 1950) Sup. 6: 55–56.

"Centre Musical Kleinhans à Buffalo." *L'Architecture d'Aujourd'hui* 20 (May 1949): 16.

"Centre Technique de la General Motors à Detroit." *L'Architecture d'Aujourd'hui* 20 (April 1950) Sup. 5: 42–44; 24 (December 1953): 49–55.

"The Chicago Tribune Building." *Architekten* 25 (February 1923): 22–27.

"Chicago Tribune Building" (editorial). *Architecture* 47 (March 1923): 87–88.

"The City." *Municipal Reference Library* 29 (October 1943): 41.

"The City: Its Growth, Its Decay, Its Future." *Architectural Record* 94 (July 1943): 26.

"*The City* by Eliel Saarinen" (book review). *Architectural Forum* 78 (June 1943): 12, 104.

"Civic Center Planned for Detroit." *Interiors* 108 (July 1949): 18.

"Columbus, Indiana; Tabernacle Church of Christ." *Architectural Forum* 77 (October 1942): 35–44.

Conroy, Sarah Booth. "Saarinen at Cranbrook: Michigan Moderne." *Horizon* 22 (March 1979): 55–59.

Couleur. "Arkitektuflykten." *Arkitekten* 7 (September 1909): 121–27.

Courtney, W. B. "There's Always Finland." *Collier's* 96 (28 December 1935): 12–13, 46–47.

"Cranbrook." *Harper's Bazaar* 72 (1 March 1939): 89–90, 119–20.

"Cranbrook Academy, Bloomfield Hills, Michigan." *Progressive Architecture* 58 (August 1977): 53.

"Cranbrook Academy of Art." *London Studio* 24 (*Studio* 124) (November 1942): 159–61.

"The Cranbrook Academy of Art." *Octagon* 6 (July 1934): 11.

"Cranbrook Academy of Art, Bloomfield Hills, Michigan." *Architectural Record* 68 (December 1930): 444–51.

"Cranbrook Academy of Art Musée et Bibliothèque." *L'Architecture d'Aujourd'hui* 20 (April 1950) Sup. 7: 57–58.

"Cranbrook Academy of Art Museum and Library." *Pencil Points* 24 (December 1943): 36–49.

"Cranbrook Academy of Art Program." *Architectural Record* 73 (June 1933): 430–31.

"Cranbrook Begins Work on New Gallery." *Museum News* 18 (1 September 1940): 1.

"Cranbrook Erecting New Museum Building: Institute of Science." *Museum News* 14 (15 June 1936): 14.

"Cranbrook Expands." *Art Digest* 17 (January 1943): 13.

"Cranbrook: An Interesting Experiment." *Magazine of Art* 22 (February 1931): 142–43.

"Cranbrook School in Bloomfield Hills." *Michigan Engineer* 59 (Convention no., 1940): 2 (photographs on cover and p. 4).

"Cranbrook School, Bloomfield Hills, Michigan." *Architectural Record* 64 (December 1928): 452–60, 475–506, 525–28, frontispiece.

"Cranbrook School—Founded on Ideals." *Magazine of the Women's City Club* (May, 1927), pp. 16–17, 28, 30.

"Cranbrook's Setting." *Art Digest* 17 (August 1943): 13.

"Cranbrook Starts Building." *Art Digest* 15 (October 15, 1940): 13.

Crane, Theodore. "The Future of American Design." *Pencil Points* 18 (October 1937): 651–58.

Creese, Walter. "Saarinen as a Catalyst in American Architecture." Address to joint session of College Art Association and the American Society of Architectural Historians at the Institute of Contemporary Art, Boston, Massachusetts, January 29, 1948.

———. "Saarinen's Tribune Design." *Society of Architectural Historians Journal* 6 (July–December 1947): 1–5.

"Crow Island School, Winnetka, Illinois, with Introduction by Carleton Washburne and Frances Presler and Comment by Joseph Hudnut." *Architectural Forum* 75 (August 1941): 79–92.

Davies, Florence. "Cranbrook Foundation." *Country Life* 68 (June 1935): 11–15, 74.

———. "Cranbrook's New Museum." *Magazine of Art* 36 (January 1943): 6–9.

"Design for Detroit." *Architectural Forum,* 79 (November 1943): 102.

"Des Moines Art Center." *Museum News* 26 (15 June 1948): 1.

"Des Moines Art Center to Open with Selected Loan Exhibition." *Art Digest* 22 (1 May 1948): 15.

"Des Moines Builds Art Center." *Art Digest* 21 (1 October 1946): 19.

"Des Moines, Iowa: A University Campus Plan under Way for Drake University." *Architectural Record* 102 (December 1947): 71–83.

"Detroit Planning Studies." *Pencil Points* 24 (December 1943): 50–63; 25 (January 1944): 59–66; 25 (February, 1944), 61–68.

Ditchy, Clair W. "Eliel Saarinen, 1873–1950." *American Institute of Architects Journal* 14 (September 1950): 112–15.

———. "Eliel Saarinen 1873–1950." *Forum* 6 (February 1951): 34–46.

Dixon, John Morris. "Columbus, Indiana, the Town That Architecture Made Famous." *Architectural Forum* 123 (December 1965): 40–49.

"Dormitory Plan in Two Versions: First and Second Willow Lodge Project near Ypsilanti." *Architectural Record* 94 (October 1943): 54–60.

Dyggve, Ejnar. "Omkring Byplanmödet." *Ingemören* 30 (29 June 1921): 395–96.

Edgar, Emil. "Nádrázi." *Stavitelské Listy* 19 (January 1923): 31–37.

"Education of the Architect." *Architectural Record* 80 (September 1936): 201–6.

"Eero Saarinen Receives His Father's Last Award, Gold Medal for the RIBA." *Architectural Record* 108 (November 1950): 194.

Église à Minneapolis." *L'Architecture d'Aujourd'hui* 21 (December 1950–January 1951): 79–83.

"Eliel Saarinen" (editorial). *Arkitekten* 7 (1923): 97.

"Eliel Saarinen." *Arkkitehti Arkitekten* 5 (1955): 69–80.

"Eliel Saarinen Chosen for British Award, 1950 Gold Medal of the RIBA." *Architectural Record* 107 (March 1950): 9.

"Eliel Saarinen, Famous Modern Designer." *Friends*, August, 1941, pp. 8–9.

"Eliel Saarinens förslag till omreglering av Lake Front området in Chicago." *Arkitekten* 4, no. 2 (1924): 15–28.

"Eliel Saarinen Receives Gold Medal for 1946." *American Institute of Architects Journal* 7 (May 1947): 230–31.

"Eliel Saarinen's Last Sketches: Campus Chapel for Stephens College at Columbia, Mo." *Progressive Architecture* 32 (June 1951): 15–16.

"Eliel Saarinen to be Awarded AIA Gold Medal for 1947." *Architectural Record* 101 (February 1947): 14.

"Eliel Saarinen to Receive the 1950 Gold Medal of the RIBA." *American Institute of Architects Journal* 13 April 1950): 167.

"Eliel Saarinen Wins AIA Gold Medal for 1946." *Architectural Forum* 86 (June 1947): 11.

Ely, Dwight P. "Eliel Saarinen—Master Architect." *Archi* 23 (June 1942): 53–56.

Englehardt, N. L. "What Can School Designers Expect?" *Pencil Points* 23 (November 1942): 46–60.

Errett, Edwin R. "A Church That Dares to Be Different." *Shane Quarterly* 4 (October 1943): 247–49.

Executive Committee, A.C.D. "Architects' Civic Design Groups of the Detroit Metropolitan Area." *Weekly Bulletin, Michigan Society of Architects* 18 (20 June 1944): 1, 4.

"Exhibition of Architecture of Saarinen, Swanson and Saarinen." *Milwaukee Gallery Notes* 19 (May 1947): 1.

Fayans, Stefan. "Baukunst und Volk." *Moderne Bauformen* 8 no. 8 (1909): 337–53, pls. 55–57.

Feiss, Carl. "Eliel Saarinen as a Teacher." *American Institute of Architects Journal* 14 (September 1950): 138–39.

Fellheimer, Alfred. "Modern Railway Passenger Terminals." *Architectural Forum* 53 (December 1930): 655–94.

"$50 Million Civic Center Is Created for Detroit." *Architectural Forum* 90 (April 1949): 12–13.

"Finland Issues Stamp Commemorating Birth of Finnish Architect Eliel Saarinen." *New York Times*, 14 October 1973, II p. 36:8.

"Finnland auf der pariser Weltausstellung." *Dekorative Kunst* 6 (September 1900): 457–65.

"FPHA Dormitories to Serve a Midwestern Bomber Plant." *Architectural Record* 92 (July 1942): 47.

Frosterus, Sigurd. "Stadsplanehärvan. *Arkitekten* 30, no. 11 (1933): 159–61.

Gatling, Eva Ingersoll. *Eliel Saarinen Memorial Exhibition*, April 15–May 6, 1951. Catalogue of the exhibition. Bloomfield Hills, Michigan: Museum of Cranbrook Academy of Art, 1951. n.p. (111 objects in exhibition). Checklist of Saarinen's works, portrait, illustrations.

"General Motors Opens First Complete Building of Technical Center." *Architectural Record* 110 (October 1951): 12.

"General Motors Technical Center." *Architectural Record* 98 (November 1945): 98–103.

"General Motors Technical Center." *Architectural Forum* 95 (November 1951): 111–23.

"General Motors Technical Center." *Architectural Forum* 98 (February 1953): 145.

"General Motors Technical Center bei Detroit, U.S.A." *Werk* 44 (February 1957): 58–64.

"General Motors Technical Centre, Detroit." *Architect and Building News* 210 (September 1956): 418–21, 427.

"Generalplanen." *Arkitekten* 30, no. 10 (1933): 143–45.

"Gesellius, Lindgren, und Saarinen." *Moderne Bauformen* 6, no. 4 (1907): 137–62, pls. 27–34.

Giedion, Sigfried. *Space, Time, and Architecture.* Cambridge: Harvard University Press, 1941. Pp. xvi+601.

"GM Center." *Interiors* 111 (November 1951): 12.

"GM City of Science and Art." *Pencil Points* 26 (September 1945): 16.

"GM Technical Center." *Architectural Record* 98 (September 1945): 16.

"GM Technical Center . . . Industrial Building in Large Groupings." *Architectural Forum* 91 (July 1949): 70–78.

Goldberger, Paul. "Bringing Back Saarinen." *New York Times*, 16 April 1978, VI:92.

Greenwood, M. "Deco 1925–1935." *Artscanada* 32, no. 4 (Winter 1975–76): 61.

Gropius, Walter. *The New Architecture and the Bauhaus.* Translated by P. Morton Shand. London: Faber & Faber, Ltd., 1935. Pp. 80+pls.

Grut, Torben A. "Den Internationella Stadsplaneafdelningen för Ordnande af ny Hufvudstad i Australien." *Arkitektur* 12 (December 1912): 141–57.

Guérard, Albert. "The Growth of Cities." *Nation* 156 (24 April 1943): 606–8.

Hamlin, Talbot. *Architecture through the Ages.* New York: G. P. Putnam's Sons, 1940. Pp. xlvii+680.

Hansen, Marika. "Gesellius—Lindgren—Saarinen vid Sekelskiftet." *Arkitekten* 9 (1967): 6–12.

Hartzog, Justin. "The City." *Landscape Architecture* 34 (October 1943): 36–37.

Harvia, Yrjö. "Eliel Saarinen, Munksnäs-Haga och Stor-Helsingfors." *Kommunaltidskrift* 1 (January 1916): 14–15.

Haskell, Douglas. "Chicago Interlude." *Architectural Forum* 116 (May 1962): 214.

H[askell,] D[ouglas]. "Eliel Saarinen, 1873–1950." *Architectural Forum* 93 (August 1950): 82–83.

Hay, Jessica Ayer. "The Story of Two Artists Who Are Designing Cranbrook School." *Afterglow* 3 (September 1927): 15–17.

Hegemann, Werner. "Das Hochhaus als Verkehrstörer und der Wettbewerb der Chicago Tribune." *Wasmuths Monatshefte für Baukunst* 8 (1924): 296–309.

"Herald-American Better Chicago Contest Winners." *Architectural Forum* 84 (January 1946): 8.

"He Thinks in Big Terms," *Afterglow* 1 (October 1925): 1, 5, 23.

Hitchcock, Henry-Russell, Jr. *Modern Architecture.* New York: Payson & Clarke, Ltd., 1929. Pp. xvii+252.

———. "Modern Architecture: The Traditionalists and the New Tradition." *Architectural Record* 63 (April 1928): 337–49.

"Homes of Yesterday and Tomorrow." *Weekly Bulletin of the Michigan Society of Architects* 7 (October 10 and 17): 1, 4.

"Honors Starred His Long Career." *Architectural Record* 108 (August 1950): 12.

Hoving, Victor. *En Wiborgare i Helsingfors och Stockholm.* Helsingfors: Söderström & Co., 1945. Pp. 301.

"How to Cure the City." *Time* 40 (20 July 1942): 48.

Howe, George. "Monuments, Memorials, and Modern Design—an Exchange of Letters." *Magazine of Art* 37 (October 1944): 202–7.

Hudnut, Joseph. "Kleinhans Music Hall, Buffalo, N.Y." *Architectural Forum* 75 (July 1941): 35–42.

———. "Recent Buildings." *House and Garden* 77 (July 1940, Sec. 1): 42–43.

———. "Sala de conciertos." *Revista de arquitectura* 26 (September 1941): 405–9. Translation of the article which appeared in *Architectural Forum*, July, 1941.

———. "Smithsonian Competition Results." *Magazine of Art* 32 (August 1939): 456–59.

Hunter, Penelope. "Art Deco and the Metropolitan Museum of Art." *Connoisseur* 179 (April 1972): 273–81.

Huxtable, Ada Louise. "Hvittrask, Art Nouveau Style House in Helsinki, Finland." *New York Times*, 13 February 1966, VI, p. 64.

"Illustration of the Work of Eliel Saarinen, Architect," *American Architect and Architectural Review* 124 (26 September 1923): 19 pls.

"Indrukken uit het noorden Groot-Helsingfors." *Bouwkundig Weekblad* 40 (25 October 1919): 262–65.

"Institute of Science Building, Cranbrook Academy, Bloomfield Hills, Michigan." *Architectural Forum* 69 (December 1938): 418–24.

International Cities and Town Planning Exhibition. Jubilee Exhibition. Gothenburg, Sweden, 1923. Pp. 389.

The International Competition for a New Administration Building for the Chicago Tribune MCMXXII. Chicago: Tribune Co., 1923. Pp. 103+283 pls.

"Internordisk Byggnadsdag." *Arkitekten* 29, no. 6 (1932): 87–89.

Jeanneret-Gris, Charles Édouard. *The City of Tomorrow.* Translated by Frederick Etchells. New York: Payson & Clarke, 1929. Pp. xxvii+301.

Johns, Orrick. "Finnish Architect Prescribes for Us." *New York Times*, May 17, 1925.

Jung, Bertel. "Eliel Saarinen," *Arkitekten* 29, no. 3 (1932): 33–43.

———. "Munksnäs-Haga och Stor-Helsingfors." *Arkitekten* 6, no. 6 (1915): 73–77; 6, no. 7 (1915): 89–92.

———. "Ode till Eliel Saarinen." *Arkitekten* 30, no. 8 (1933): 31.

———. *Pro Helsingfors.* Helsingfors: Lilius & Hertzberg, 1918.

———. *Suur-Helsinki.* Helsinki: Lilius & Hertzberg, 1918. Pp. 18.

Kalevala, The Land of Heroes. Translated from original Finnish by W. F. Kirby. Everyman's Library No. 259–60 (First published in this edition 1907). London: Dent; New York: Dutton [1923–25]. 2 v. (xvi, 327, 285p.).

Kalevalatalo. Helsinki: Kalevalaseura, Otava, 1921. Pp. 14+11 pls.

"Kalevalatalo." *Arkkitehti* 11–12 (1943): 46–50.

Kallio, Oiva. "Generalplanen för Helsingfors." *Arkitekten* 30, no. 8 (1933): 111–12.

Kelsey, Albert. *The Monumental Lighthouse.* Pan-American Union, 1930. Pp. 187.

Kershner, Frederick D. "Saarinen's Triumph." *Shane Quarterly* 4 (October 1943): 250–51.

"Keskustela Helsingista" *Arkkitehti* 71, no. 1 (1975): 25–60.

Killam, Charles W. "Questions for Planners." *Architectural Record* 94 (August 1943): 30–31, 96–98.

Kin, W. "Taidekirjallisuutta." *Valvoja* 36 (February 1916): 137–40.

"The Kingswood School for Girls, Cranbrook, Michigan." *Architectural Forum* 56 (January 1932): 37–60.

Kleinhans Music Hall. With Foreword by Edward H. Letchworth. "The Dream" by Alice Tierney Scanlan; "The Design" by Eliel Saarinen; "The Acoustics" by Charles C. Potwin; "Comment" by Joseph Hudnut; "The Lighting" by Stanley McCandless; "The Management" by Winifred Eaton Corey. Buffalo: Kleinhans Music Hall Management, Inc., 1942.

"Kleinhans Music Hall, Buffalo." *Architectural Forum* 75 (July 1941): 35–42.

"Kleinhans Music Hall, Buffalo," p. 47, in *Guide to Modern Architecture, Northeast States.* New York: Museum of Modern Art, 1940.

Kulkija. "Suurenmoinen suunnitelma." *Naisten Ääni* 16 (13 August 1921): 163–65.

"La Maison—Témoin du 1900 Finlandais." *Connaissance des Arts* 238 (December 1971): 108–13, 192.

La Marre, Linda. "Restoring to Saarinen That Which Is Saarinen's." *Detroit News*, 7 May 1978, 1C, 14C.

"Lapsuusmuistojen Maailma." *Uutta Kylvöä* (1929), pp. 32–59.

Laurin, Carl G. *Konsthistoria.* Stockholm: P. A. Norstedt & Son, 1901. Pp. 703.

Leipziger, Hugo. *The Architectonic City in the Americas.* Austin: University of Texas, 1944. Pp. 68+40 pls.

———. *Distinctness versus Vagueness: The Ecological Problem of the Modern City.* Austin: University of Texas, 1944. Pp. 61+40 pls.

Lindberg, Carolus. "Eliel Saarinen." *Builder* 125 (10 August 1923): 200–205, 209.

———. "Ragnar Östberg och hans stadshus." *Arkitekten* 7 (1923): 99–103.

Looyen Joh. D. "Herinneringen Tentoonstelling Leipzig 1913." *Bouwkundig Weekblad* 34 (18 April 1914): 185–86+2 pls.

"Maailman Kaunein Talo." *Suomen Kuvalehti* 50–51 (December 1922): 1267.

Macomber, Henry P. "The Michigan Home of Eliel Saarinen." *House Beautiful* 74 (October 1933): 133–36.

Meier-Graefe, Julius. "Die Kultur Finnlands." *Die neue Rundschau* 16 (April 1905): 486–501.

Memorial Hall: A Report Made by Detroit City Council, June, 1924. Pp. 1–13. Pamphlet.

"Metropolis. 1. New York: Un Mythe Européen. Part 2. Trois Architectes Européen en Amerique: Eliel Saarinen, Mendelsohn, Neutra," *Archithese* (entire issue), no. 17 (1976).

Meurman, Otto I. *Asemakaavaoppi.* Helsinki: Otava, 1947. Pp. 460.

———. "Eliel Saarinen," *Kulkuset*, December, 1920, pp. 21–25.

———. "Helsingfors Generalplan." *Arkitekten* 31, no. 4 (1934): 59–60.

———. "Munkinniemen-Haaga ja Suur-Helsinki." *Teknillinen Aikakauslehti* 10 (October 1915): 149–54.

———. "Munkkinieme ja Haaga." *Otava* 11 (November 1915): 505–12.

———. "Städtebaufragen in Finnland." *Der Städtebau* 22 (1927): 165–73.

Mies van der Rohe, Ludwig. "A Tribute to Frank Lloyd Wright." *College Art Journal* 6 (Autumn 1946): 41.

Miller, Hugh Th. "To Our Visitors." *Shane Quarterly* 4 (October 1943): 244–46.

Miller, Nory. "Exploring the Fundamentals in Fundamentalist Columbus, Indiana." *Inland Architect* 16, no. 10 (December 1972): 9–13.

"Milwaukee's Proposed Memorial Center." *Architectural Record* 102 (November 1947): 74–77.

"Minneapolis: Christ Church." *Architectural Forum* 93 (July 1950): 80–85.

Mock, Elizabeth and Rudolf. "Schools Are for Children." In: *American School and University*, pp. 37–42. New York: American School Pub. Corp., 1943.

"Modern Features of Art," *Pencil Points* 10 (March 1929): 202.

Morrison, Hugh. *Louis Sullivan, Prophet of Modern Architecture.* New York: W. W. Norton & Co., 1935. Pp. xxi+391.

Moses, Robert. "The Long-haired Planners." *New York Times*, June 25, 1944, VI, p. 16:2.

Mujica, Francisco. *History of the Skyscraper.* Paris: Archaeology and Architecture Press, 1929. Pp. 72+134 pls.

"Munksnäs-Haga." *Arkitekten* 19 (January 1917): 129–32.

"Munksnäs-Nytt." *Veckans Krönika* 49 (4 December 1920): 1151.

Muthesius, Hermann. "Die Bedeutung des Kunstgewerbes." *Dekorative Kunst* 10 (February 1907): 177–92.

"New General Motors Technical Production Center." *Architect and Engineer* 163 (October 1945): 12.

"Nice Space: The Cranbrook Campus, 1924–1943." *Space Design* no. 134 (October 1975): 99–105. [Japanese text; English summaries]

Nichols, Ashton. "Looking at Books." Book Review of *Unbuilt America. Preservation News* 17 (May 1977): 9.

Niilonen, Kerttu. "Arkkitehtuuri." *Kuva*, September, 1946, pp. 4–6.

North, Arthur T. "The Passing Show." *Current Architecture* 40 (March 1931): 15–16, 21.

"Not of One Mind." *American Architect and Architecture* 149 (December 1936): 17–27.

Nyström, Per. *Tolv kapitel om Munksnäs.* Helsinki: Söderström & Co., 1945. Pp. 175.

Öhquist, Johannes. "Eliel Saarinen." *Aamu*, December, 1929, pp. 333–42, 346–47.

———. "Ein finnischer Städtebauer." *Der Städtebau* 17, nos. 3/4 (1920): 21–27, pls. 13–19.

———. *Finnland.* Berlin: Kurt Vowinckel, 1928. Pp. x+256.

———. *Samtida konst i Finland.* Malmö, Sweden: John Kroon, A. B. Malmö Ljustrycksanstalt, 1929. Pp. 192.

———. *Suomen Taiteen Historia.* Helsinki: Weilin & Göös, 1912. Pp. 666.

Osman, M. E. "25-Year Award to a Classic Church." *American Institute of Architects Journal* 66 (May 1977): 28–29.

Östberg, Ragnar. "Finlands nya Landtdagshus." *Arkitektur och Dekorativ Konst* 28 (April 1908): 41–44.

"Opera Shed." *Progressive Architecture (Pencil Points)* 28 (March 1947): 53–58.

Osborn. "Review of *The City,*" *Town and Country Planning*, August, 1944.

Osborn, Max. "Ein modernes märkisches Waldschlösschen." *Moderne Bauformen* 7, no. 6 (1908): 219–39.

Osborne, Milton S. "Cranbrook Academy of Art." *Archi* 23 (June 1942): 59.

Osthaus, Karl Ernst. "Der Bahnhof." *Der Verkehr.* Jena: Eugen Diederichs, 1914. Pp. 122.

"Our Biggest Art Problem." *American Artist* 7 (September 1943): 24–25, 34.

Parker, Paul. "Des Moines Opens Community Art Center." *Art Digest* 22 (July 1948): 9–10.

Parmala, H. "Suur-Helsinki." *Helsingin Kaiku* 13 (19 November 1915): 379–84.

Paulsen, Glen. "Detroit: Virile or Anemic?" *American Institute of Architects Journal* 55 (June 1971): 39–40.

"Piety in Brick." *Time* 37 (27 January 1941): 39–40.

Pond, Irving K. "High Buildings and Beauty," Parts I and II. *Architectural Forum* 38 (February 1923): 41–45; 38 (April 1923), 179–82.

"Post-war Plan for General Motors Laboratory." *Architectural Forum* 82 (August 1945): 7.

"Preserving the Recent Past." *Progressive Architecture* 55 (July 1974): 48–79, 96–103.

"Profession of Architecture." *American Architect and Architecture* 149 (December 1936): 18.

"Professori Eliel Saarisen Kodista." *Suomen Kuvalehti* 15 (19 September 1931): 1532–33 and cover.

"Proposed Pavilion Designed for Summer Symphonic Festivals." *Architectural Record* 85 (January 1939): 44–45.

Rank, Otto. *Art and Artist.* New York: Alfred A. Knopf, 1932. Pp. xxvii+431+xii.

Reid, Kenneth. "Eliel Saarinen—Master of Design," *Pencil Points* 17 (September 1936): 463–94.

"Report of the Jury [Frederic A. Delano, John A. Holabird, Walter Gropius, George Howe, Henry R. Shipley]." *Architectural Forum* 71 (July 1939): i, ii.

Rich, Lorimer. "A Study in Contrasts." *Pencil Points* 22 (August 1941): 497–516.

———. "Search for Form." *Progressive Architecture* 29 (November 1948): 114–20.

Richards, James Maude. "Hvitträsk." *Architectural Review* 139 (February 1966): 152–54.

Rivard, Nancy J. "Eliel Saarinen in America." M.A. thesis, Wayne State University, 1973. 147p. Bibliography.

Robertson, Howard. "Eliel Saarinen, the Royal Gold Medallist, 1950." *Architect and Building News* 197 (27 January 1950): 82–83.

Rönnberg, Hanna. "Konstnärshemmet vid Hvitträsk." *Hemma och Ute* 3 (August 1913): 210–14.

———. "Munksnäs-Haga Utställningen i Riddarhuset." *Hemma och Ute* 5 (15 November 1915): 302–3.

"Room for a Lady, 1934, and Dining Room, 1929." *Architectural Forum* 61 (December 1934): 412–13.

"Royal Gold Medal for Architecture, 1950." *Royal Institute of British Architects Journal* 57 (February 1950): 126.

Ryder, Sharon Lee. "Interior Design: Saarinen Atelier." *Progressive Architecture* 55 (July 1974): 70–75.

"Saarinen Advanced to Fellowship." *American Institute of Architects Journal* 2 (August 1944): 83.

The Saarinen Door: Eliel Saarinen, Architect and Designer at Cranbrook. With Foreword by Henry S. Booth. Introduction by Eva Ingersoll Gatling. Reprint of Saarinen's A.I.A. address (April 1931), "My Point of View of Our Contemporary Architecture." Bloomfield Hills, Michigan: Cranbrook Academy of Art, 1963. 64p.

Saarinen, Eero. *Eero Saarinen on His Work: A Selection of Buildings Dating from 1947 to 1964.* With statements by the architect. Edited by Aline B. Saarinen. New Haven and London: Yale University Press, 1962. 108 p.

"Saarinen: Royal Gold Medallist." *The Builder* 178 (27 January 1950): 125–26.

"Saarinen's Andirons." *Craft Horizons* 35 (February 1975): 24.

Schroderus, Eino. "Eliel Saarinen Purjehduskaudelta, 1873–1933." *Arkitekten* 30, no. 8 (1933): 31.

Schur, Ernst. "Des Haus Molchow bei Altruppin." *Dekorative Kunst* 11 (June 1908): 377–92.

Schwagermann, C. H. "Het aesthetisch Gedeelte van Stedenbouw." *Bouwkundig Weekblad* 34 (25 April 1914): 198–202.

Setälä, Helmi, *Kun Suuret Olivat Pieniä.* Helsinki: Kustannusosakeyhtiö Otava, 1911. Pp. 250.

"70 against the World." *Time* 49 (17 March 1947): 54.

Shay, Howell Lewis. "Modern Architecture and Tradition," Parts I and II. *T-Square Club Journal of Philadelphia* 1 (January 1931): 15; 1 (February 1931), 13–14.

Sherman, Roger Wade. "The Art of City Building." *American Architect* 147 (October 1935): 12–20.

Sive, André. "Urbanisme américaine." *L'Architecture d'Aujourd'hui,* 1946, pp. 106–8.

"Six Recent Buildings in the U.S.A.: General Motors Technical Center Near Detroit." *The Architect's Yearbook* 5 (1953): 133–69.

Sky, Alison, and Stone, Michelle. *Unbuilt America.* New York: McGraw-Hill, 1976. 308 p.

"Skyskraparetävlan i Chicago" (editorial). *Byggnads-Tidningen* 14, no. 3 (1923): 33–39.

Smith, T. K. "Tabernacle Church of Christ." *Shane Quarterly* 4 (October 1943): 252–57.

"Smithsonian Art Gallery Design Prize to Saarinen." *Museum News* 17 (1 September 1939): 1.

"Smithsonian Competition Results." *Magazine of Art* 32 (August 1939): 456–59, 488–89.

"The Smithsonian Gallery of Art Competition." *Architectural Forum* 71 (July 1939): i–xvi.

"So You're Going to Plan a City." *Fortune* 29 (January 1944): 123–25, 172, 174, 177, 178, 180, 183.

"Stadtplanung für Reval." *Der Städtebau* 18, no. 5/6, 45–46.

Stephen, J. Davidson. "Detroit and the Detroit Area," Parts I and II (with introduction by Eliel Saarinen). *New Pencil Points* 24 (December 1943): 36–49; 25 (January 1944): 59–66.

Stephenson, Gordon. "Two Important Books on Planning." *Journal of the Royal Institute of British Architects* 50 (October 1943): 285–86.

Strengell, Gustaf. "L'Architecte Eliel Saarinen." *L'Art vivant* 92 (15 October 1928): 794, 800–801.

———. *Byggnaden som Konstverk.* Hellsingfors: Holger Schildts Förlag, 1928. Pp. 163.

———. "Kingswood School." *Suomen Kuvalehti* 16 (7 May 1932): 692–93.

———. "Mihin Eliel Saarisen 'Suur-Helsinki'—ehdotus tähtää." *Suomen Kuvalehti* 15 (5 December 1931): 28–31.

———. "Mitä Eliel Saarinen on viime aikoina toiminut Amerikassa." *Kansan Kuvalehti* 6 (12 February 1932): 4–6.

Sullivan, Louis Henry. *Autobiography of an Idea.* New York: Press of the American Institute of Architects, 1924. Pp. 329.

———. "The Chicago Tribune Competition," *Architectural Record* 53 (February 1923): 151–57.

———. *Kindergarten Chats.* Edited by Claude F. Bragdon. Lawrence, Kan.: Scarab Fraternity Press, 1934. Pp. xi+256.

"Summer at Cranbrook." *Art Digest* 7 (July 1933): 14.

Swanson, J. Robert F. "Eliel Saarinen." *Michigan Technic* 37 (May 1924): 4–6.

Swartwout, Egerton. "Review of Recent Architectural Magazines." *American Architect and Architectural Review* 123 (20 June 1923): 574–78.

Tallmadge, Thomas E. *The Story of Architecture in America.* New York: W. W. Norton & Co., 1927. Pp. 303.

"Tanglewood Opera House." *Architectural Review* 101 (May 1947): 163–64.

"Théatre Lyrique du Centre Musical de Berkshire." *L'Architecture d'Aujourd'hui* 20 (May 1949): 19–21.

Thomé, Valter. "Eliel Saarinen och Stor-Helsingfors." *Nya Argus* 22 (November 1915): 199–200.

Tikkanen, J. J. "Die dekorative Kunst in Finnland." *Die Kunst* 4 (January 1903): 121–60+2 color pls.

———. "Gesellius, Lindgren, und Saarinen." *Innen-Dekoration* 14 (December 1903): 289–306.

Tilghman, Donnell. "Eliel Saarinen." *Architectural Record* 63 (May 1928): 393–402.

Tselos, Dimitri Theodore. "Richardson's Influence on European Architecture." *Society of Architectural Historians Journal* 29 (May 1970): 156–62.

Välikangas, Martti. "Nordisk Byggnadsdags Utställningar." *Arkitekten* 29, no. 7 (1932): 102–3.

"Var Stad." *Pro Helsingfors.* Helsingfors: Holger Schildts Förlag. Pp. 396.

Varming, K. "Det tredie nordiske Arkitektmöde." *Arkitekten* 11 (July 1909): 493–500.

Vikman, Rita. "Eräs Koti." *Suomen Kuvalehti* 12 (7 July 1928): 1215–17.

"Vittorp—ett ungdomsverk av Eliel Saarinen." *Astra* 15 (September 1933): 348–50.

Vogt, Von Ogden. *Art and Religion.* Boston: Beacon Press, 1948. Pp. 297.

Von Eckardt, Wolf. "The Cranbrook Academy of Art." *New Republic* 178 (24 June 1978): 27–30.

Wattjes, J. G. *Moderne Architectuur.* Amsterdam: Maatschappij Kosmos, 1927. Pp. 307.

Wennervirta, L. *Finlands Konst.* Helsingfors: Söderström & Co., 1926. Pp. 631.

Wernekke. "Der Wettbewerb um einen Bebauungsplan für die Bundeshauptstadt von Australien." *Der Städtebau* 10, no. 7 (1913): 73–77, 86–88.

"What Place Art in the Post-War World?" *Art Digest* 17 (August 1943): 12.

"Willow Run Town Center." *Architectural Forum* 78 (March 1943): 38–41.

"Winners of Smithsonian Gallery of Art Competition." *Architectural Record* 86 (August 1939): 50.

"Winnetka Kindergarten and Elementary School." *Architectural Record* 91 (January 1942): 3–4.

Woltersdorf, Arthur. *Living Architecture*. Chicago: A. Kroch, 1930. Pp. 178+12 pls.

Wright, Frank Lloyd. *An Autobiography*. New York: Longmans, Green & Co., 1932. Pp. 371+pls.

———. *Modern Architecture*. Princeton: Princeton University Press, 1931. Pp. 115.

Munksnäs-Haga. With "Stadsplanskonst" by Gustaf Strengell. Helsingfors: Lilius & Hertzberg, 1915. Pp. 123 with additional photographs and diagrams.

"Stadtplanung für Reval." *Der Städtebau* 18, nos. 5/6 (1921): 45–56, pls. 21–26.

"Project for Lake Front Development of the City of Chicago." *American Architect and Architectural Review* 124 (5 December 1923): 487–514. (Copyright, 1923, Architectural and Building Press, Inc.)

The Cranbrook Development. (An address by Saarinen given at the American Institute of Architects convention, San Antonio, Texas, April, 1931). Privately printed.

"My Point of View of Our Contemporary Architecture." *Architectural Progress* 5 (August 1931): 7–13, 24. (Reprinted from *Octagon.*) This is the last part of an address delivered at a convention of the American Institute of Architects, San Antonio, Texas, April, 1931. The complete address is reprinted in *The Saarinen Door,* pp. 56–60. See also "The Principles of Modern Architecture," below.

"Lausunto Eräistä Helsingin Kaupungin Asemakaavakysmyksistä." *Helsingin Kaupungin Keskiosien Yleisasemakaavaehdotus.* Helsingissä, 1932. Liite. Pp. 1–70.

"The Principles of Modern Architecture." *Royal Institute of British Architects Journal* 39 (January 1932): 235–39. This is a reprint of an address delivered at a convention of the American Institute of Architects, San Antonio, Texas, April 1931. See also "My Point of View of Our Contemporary Architecture," above.

"Architecture in the Post-war World." *Art Digest* 17 (August 1943): 12.

The City: Its Growth—Its Decay—Its Future. New York: Reinhold Pub., 1943. Pp. 377. Reviewed in *American Artist* 7 (September 1943): 24–25; *Architectural Forum* 78 (June 1943): 12, 104; *Architectural Record* 94 (July 1943): 26; *Architectural Review* 94 (August 1943): 30; *Journal of Aesthetics* 3, no. 11 (1945): 87; *Landscape Architecture* 34 (October 1943): 36–37; *Liturgical Arts* 12 (November 1943): 16; *Municipal Reference Library* 29 (October 1943): 41; *The Nation* 156 (24 April 1943): 606–8; *Octagon* 15 (June 1943): 33; *Royal Institute of British Architects Journal* 50 (3 October 1943): 283–85; *Town and Country Planning,* August 1944.

"Eliel Saarinen Receives the Gold Medal—The Citation and Mr. Saarinen's Response at the Seventy-ninth Convention, Grand Rapids, April 30, 1947." *Journal of the American Institute of Architects* 7 (June 1947): 284–88.

Search for Form. New York: Reinhold Pub., 1948. Pp. xxi+351. Reviewed in *Architectural Record* 104 (August 1948): 28; *Architectural Review* 105 (April 1949): 199; *L'Architecture d'Aujourd'hui* 19 (December 1948): xxi; *Burlington Magazine* 92 (February 1950): 59; *College Art Journal* 9, no. 3 (1950): 362–63; *Interiors* 108 (November 1948): 18; *Progressive Architecture* 29 (November 1948): 114–20; *Royal Institute of British Architects Journal* 58 (December 1950): 69.

"The Royal Gold Medal 1950; Message from Eliel Saarinen, Royal Gold Medalist, with Illustrations of Some of His Work." *Royal Institute of British Architects Journal* 57 (April 1950): 216–17.

ACKNOWLEDGMENTS

To Eliel *and* Loja Saarinen, *who, patiently and conscientiously, gave months of their time and a good deal of effort to the development of this book.*

To Alvar Aalto *for his thoughtful Foreword to this biography of his friend and colleague.*

To Joseph Hudnut *and* Eero Saarinen *for reading the manuscript and giving invaluable advice concerning the factual and interpretive material in this volume.*

To Douglas Haskell, *whose sound judgment and helpful advice greatly aided in the shaping of the new edition.*

To Joseph N. Lacy, *whose personal knowledge of the organization of the various Saarinen architectural firms added immeasurably to the accuracy of this edition.*

To Professor Heikki Sirén *for permission to quote the words spoken by his father,* Professor J. S. Sirén, *at the opening of the Eliel Saarinen Memorial Exhibition in Helsinki, June 1, 1955.*

To Harold Nelson, *whose interest in the work of Eliel Saarinen and in the publication of this biography never failed. His efforts have been truly appreciated.*

To Mr. *and* Mrs. Fairfax Cone, *whose generous financial assistance enabled the publication of this volume to proceed in spite of long delay and rising costs.*

To my wife, Virginia Morgan Christ-Janer, *and to* Christopher Morris, Eugenia Hrones, Ruth Virginia Sheehan, *and* Virginia Ball *for their faithful work in research, proofreading, and typing.*

To the director and staff of the Museum of Finnish Architecture for their permission to use and their help in assembling the illustrations for the later edition.

To the members of the administrative and teaching staffs of Cranbrook Academy of Art who, through a span of thirty years and two editions, have supplied assistance of several kinds.

To the photographers, authors, editors, designers, and publishers who have, in various ways, contributed to this book.

163

ELIEL SAARINEN
Bronze bust by Loja Saarinen

IN MEMORIAM

Eliel Saarinen rounded out a fruitful and orderly career at the age of 76 as an architect and planner of the Twentieth Century. His life was a measured, loyal and filial kind of life, leavened with wit and courtesy; his work is a profoundly considered and soundly wholesome work, done with unstinting care and studied originality.

Douglas Haskell, Editor
Architectural Forum
October, 1950